**Determann's Field Guide to
Artificial Intelligence Law**

Elgar Compliance Guides

For a full list of Edward Elgar published titles, including the titles in this series, visit our website at www.e-elgar.com.

Determann's Field Guide to Artificial Intelligence Law

International Corporate Compliance

LOTHAR DETERMANN

Baker McKenzie LLP, Palo Alto, USA; Freie Universität Berlin, Germany; University of California, Berkeley School of Law, USA

Elgar Compliance Guides

Edward Elgar PUBLISHING

Cheltenham, UK • Northampton, MA, USA

Published by
Edward Elgar Publishing Limited
The Lypiatts
15 Lansdown Road
Cheltenham
Glos GL50 2JA
UK

Edward Elgar Publishing, Inc.
William Pratt House
9 Dewey Court
Northampton
Massachusetts 01060
USA

A catalogue record for this book
is available from the British Library

Library of Congress Control Number: 2023949803

This book is available electronically in the **Elgar**online
Law subject collection
http://dx.doi.org/10.4337/9781035326969

ISBN 978 1 0353 2695 2 (cased)
ISBN 978 1 0353 2696 9 (eBook)
ISBN 978 1 0353 3100 0 (paperback)

Printed and bound in Great Britain by
TJ Books Limited, Padstow, Cornwall

Content overview

Contents

About Your Guide

In one of my earliest childhood memories, I am playing under my father's desk at home with rectangular cards in green, red, white, and blue that contained dozens of lines of oval holes at different intervals. Later, my father explained that the holes in these punch cards represented instructions to a very large mainframe computer in the form of ones and zeros, current and no current, the only signals the computer processed. In the 1960s and 1970s, he wrote early computer programs to optimize shapes for optical lenses and mirrors in microscopes made by Ernst Leitz GmbH in Wetzlar, then a family-owned business that is famous also for its Leica (short for "**Lei**tz **ca**mera") products. My father read many science fiction books to me, including *I, Robot* by Isaac Asimov, as well as Robert Jungk's books about the development of the nuclear bomb and other dangerous new technologies, including *The Future Has Already Begun*. He also gave me an early hand-held Hewlett Packard calculator and later a Commodore home computer and taught me basic programming.

I grew up in a country (Germany) that produced many technical innovations, but that also held a deep-seated fear of adverse effects of new technologies. Around the time I was born, my home state of Hessen passed the world's first data protection law, a predecessor to the European Union's General Data Protection Regulation (GDPR), due to fears of civil rights abuses by the police fighting domestic terrorism. In 1990, an appeals court in the town of Kassel issued a preliminary injunction prohibiting gene technology development in Germany until the federal parliament enacted legislation to address potential risks. With similar reasoning, German courts started issuing preliminary injunctions in 1993 against the construction of mobile phone stations due to fears of "Electrosmog," which I examined in my 1996 doctoral thesis on "New, potentially dangerous technologies as a legal problem."

In 1999, I qualified for tenure as a law professor with my post-doctoral thesis on "Freedom of Communications on the Internet" at the Free University of Berlin, where I have been teaching since 1994. I moved to San Francisco to practice technology law at the international law firm Baker McKenzie and started teaching Computer Law at the University of San Francisco School of Law and at the University of California, Berkeley School of Law, addressing AI-related questions, among many other information technology-related topics.

In my law practice, I have been advising numerous companies, from start-ups to tech giants, on the development, commercialization, and use of new technologies, often long before specific laws, regulations, or court decisions provided clear rules on compliance requirements. I have developed privacy impact assessment forms, external code usage guidelines, and risk review processes for clients since the early 2000s, years before companies became statutorily required to document data protection impact assessments under the GDPR. Here, too, AI-related questions have come up from time to time over the years, but AI's practical implications seemed remote and futuristic to most clients until recently.

When OpenAI launched ChatGPT at the end of 2022 and attracted 100 million users around the world in less than two months, AI became top of mind for nearly everyone, jumped to front pages of the media, and became a staple item on political and corporate agendas. Public and private sector organizations alike rushed to inquire about opportunities, risks, and legal compliance requirements.

With this *Field Guide to Artificial Intelligence Law*, I hope to provide practical guidance to attorneys, compliance officers, engineers, privacy professionals, and other company representatives. I adopted a similar approach in 2010 when I came up with my *Field Guide to Data Privacy Law*, which is now available in its 5th edition in English and also in a dozen other languages around the world. I included high-level guidance on privacy-related topics concerning AI in my *Field Guide to Data Privacy Law*, but I believe that AI raises many more pressing legal compliance issues, which I am addressing in this book. Just as any explorer of a new area of nature benefits from a field guide identifying flora, fauna, and trails, I am hoping you will find this *Field Guide to AI Law* helpful for navigating complex problems at the intersection of technology, law, and international corporate compliance.

A number of scholars, clients, colleagues, students, friends, and family members made valuable contributions to this guide. I am particularly grateful to Jessica Vapnek, Professor of Practice at the University of California College of the Law, San Francisco; Ken Caldeira, Senior Scientist at Breakthrough Energy and Carnegie Institution for Science; Ashley Pantuliano, Associate General Counsel, OpenAI; Dan Ralls, Global Legal Counsel, TikTok; Carla J. "CJ" Utter, Privacy Counsel, Xperi, Inc.; Pamela Church, Helena Engfeldt, and Irina Shestakova, partners at Baker McKenzie; Ruth Hill Bro, Special Advisor, ABA Cybersecurity Legal Task Force and past Chair, ABA Science & Technology Law Section; Frances Say, legal assistant at Baker McKenzie; Anne Determann; Martin Determann, Automotive Engineer; Dr. Hans Determann, physicist; Garima Kedia, LLM Candidate 2024, University of California, Berkeley School of Law; Yanshu Zhang, JD Candidate 2024, The George Washington University Law School. Any errors and omissions are my own sole responsibility. Opinions expressed herein reflect my personal views, and should not be imputed to my contributors, universities, law firm, clients, or others.

Happy trails,

Lothar Determann

Orientation

This Field Guide is intended to help you navigate a complex field of laws, rights, risks, opportunities, and technology. Generalists in corporate legal departments and private practice, product counsels, compliance officers, programmers, privacy officers, data scientists, information security specialists, marketing managers, recruiters, human resources (HR) specialists, and others are confronted with artificial intelligence (AI) and related legal compliance concerns more and more frequently. A lot of information is publicly available, much of which is free of charge. Still, it can be difficult to get a handle on a practical problem quickly without getting lost in hype, political activism, advocacy, and minutiae.

That is where this Field Guide comes into play. It is designed to help identify issues, provide a brief practical overview, shape questions, and lead to solutions. It is not about "roughing it." Where the Field Guide cannot provide an answer that is detailed enough, it contains directions to further resources that are easily accessible – by providing key terminology that can be easily looked up. You will not find any footnotes with citations in "Bluebook format"; this book is for use in the field, not in a library.

In this Field Guide, you will find checklists and task lists with key compliance requirements and practical suggestions on how to go about satisfying them in an efficient manner. You will also be presented with examples of jurisdiction-specific details that global companies are most likely to encounter in the field, selected for illustrative purposes, but never for all 190+ countries. Once you have your bearings and you want to examine applicable details by country and situation, you should find it easier to research specifics.

Consider a few suggestions on how to use the Field Guide: If you got this book because you are tasked with designing or implementing a new AI law compliance program, you could start with the following overview of "Key Terms" and "Landscape" for orientation, and then use the main seven Chapters of the Field Guide for navigation. If you just want to get a quick read on a particular issue, you could look up key words in the Index at the end of the book to zoom in on a topic of particular concern. However you use this Field Guide, I hope you find it helpful as you navigate this complex and novel area of law and compliance.

Key terms

I designed the following terms and definitions for this Field Guide to convey legally relevant concepts and distinctions simply and intuitively while computer scientists, philosophers, and policymakers are still very actively debating principles and terminology. You will find additional definitions, terms, and considerations in the immediately following segment describing the Landscape.

Anthropomorphism means the attribution of human characteristics or behavior to animals, plants, or machines, for example, referring to "machine learning" or "hallucinations" relating to AI.

In this Field Guide and in my practice, I am trying to avoid anthropomorphism. We can sometimes understand novel technological concepts more quickly if we use metaphors, but lawyers and policymakers should be very careful in this respect. To preserve and protect humanity, we humans should generally distinguish between us and machines. We need to retain our ability to turn machines off without worrying whether this constitutes murder, particularly for AI that we cannot fully predict, understand, or control. We may lose this ability if we anthropomorphize too much.

Artificial Intelligence (AI) means computer systems that generate text, images, solutions to problems, and other output, functioning with substantial autonomy and in ways that their developers cannot predict, explain, or control with certainty.

Deterministic systems means computer systems that humans program with specific step-by-step instructions (if this happens, then do that...) to produce output that developers can predict, explain, and control.

This Field Guide uses "deterministic" to refer to systems that do not qualify as AI according to the immediately preceding definition. Alternative names for these types of computer systems could be rule-based, static, or traditional computing. All software is prone to malfunction due to bugs and other errors. Developers can find and fix faults in deterministic systems with patches, updates, and upgrades.

Developer means a company or individual who creates AI, typically by configuring hardware supplied by third parties, writing or modifying programming code, acquiring training data, and applying machine- and reinforced learning techniques.

Input means prompts and other information that humans submit or that AI acquires through sensors, including numbers typed on a calculator, prompts to chatbots, voice commands to smart speakers, and steering wheel movements in cars.

Output means the results of computing operations that AI provides to human operators or other systems, including numbers returned by calculators, responses from chatbots, music played by smart speakers, and directions followed by cars.

Provider means a company that hosts and maintains AI and offers users remote access to that AI's functionality, for example, via website or mobile app that delivers online chats, computer-generated images, or search results.

User means an individual or a company that obtains output from AI.

The Landscape

In this part of the Field Guide, I provide an overview regarding the field, taxonomy, territory, and key concepts. I also explain key definitions used throughout this book.

The Field

As of October 2023, no government had yet enacted any statutes or regulations that are called "artificial intelligence law" and comprehensively regulate artificial intelligence (AI). But, developers, providers, and users of AI have already been facing new challenges and interpretive problems under a wide range of existing laws, including those covering anti-discrimination, product safety, intellectual property, data protection, and other areas. Novel AI law issues are raised because of the substantial autonomy in which AI operates and the fact that developers cannot predict, explain, or control AI output with certainty. You can find an overview of key areas of AI law in Chapter 1 of this Field Guide.

Taxonomy

To identify unfamiliar species is one of the main reasons people consult nature field guides. Identifying AI in the field is a particular challenge, because we cannot rely on instincts or visual cues. We deal with automation in many forms and situations every day and cannot always easily tell whether a human, a traditionally programmed computer, or AI is directing a particular machine, communication, or other interaction. AI may be steering autonomous cars on the road, answering phone calls, responding to online chat queries, powering mobile apps, delivering Internet search results, identifying passengers via facial recognition at airports, and directing robots that mow our lawns or vacuum-clean our apartments.

Another challenge to identifying AI in the field is that not everyone agrees on what AI is and how to refer to computer systems that do not qualify as AI. Definitions and terminologies are evolving as quickly as AI itself. In this Field Guide, I refer to "Artificial Intelligence" or "AI" to mean computer systems that generate text, images, solutions to problems, and other output, functioning with substantial autonomy and in ways that their developers cannot predict, explain, or control with certainty. I refer to other computer systems as "deterministic systems," because humans program such systems with predetermined and specific step-by-step instructions (if this happens, then do that...) to produce output that developers can predict, explain, and control. The focus on predictability, explainability, and control is crucial for legal compliance purposes.

Policymakers, scientists, investors, marketing professionals, and others may prefer narrower or broader definitions for "AI" in different contexts and depending on their agenda. For example, EU regulators have been trying to restrict many forms of data processing for decades with data protection laws and other regulations. They are currently pushing for very broad definitions of "AI" in the draft EU AI Act to address perceived risks of harm that can emanate from almost any computer system. Also, entrepreneurs and marketing professionals are stretching the limits of what should reasonably pass for AI, to attract investors and buyers. Some researchers, on the other hand, propose narrower definitions, because they want to limit and delay regulation and preserve freedom to operate as long as possible.

All can very plausibly refer to common language meanings to justify broader or narrower definitions. We humans call "artificial" any things we create or invent – as opposed to "natural" things that we discover in nature. We call persons, animals, and machines "intelligent" if they are good at solving problems with something other than natural raw force, be it intuition, street smarts, analytical prowess, or sheer processing power. Therefore, one can justify expanding the definition of AI to any system that can solve problems susceptible to being addressed with human reasoning, especially when it can solve them as well as or better than humans. This, however, would also include pocket calculators.

One can narrow the definition and consider as AI only systems with sufficient generality to be able to solve as many different kinds of problems as humans are able to solve. This, however, would require AI to have a physical body and sensors to directly perceive the world. Some associate such a high definitional bar with the terms "General AI" or "AGI."

Alan Turing proposed a test in 1950 whereby a machine qualifies as intelligent if a human perceives its written output as equivalent to and indistinguishable from written responses that a human would give to the same question. With this definition, however, we would narrowly focus on a system's capability to solve only one particular problem, and not even a particularly noble one, namely, to deceive humans.

With such broader, narrower, or problem-specific definitions, we cannot focus efficiently on the particular and novel legal problems that are caused by the substantial autonomy of computer systems created with machine-learning techniques and the associated loss of predictability, explainability, and control for us humans. If we adopt overly broad definitions, we bring too many systems into the scope of AI-focused compliance requirements. This could overwhelm organizations and detract from efforts to address the greatest risks of harm. Problems associated with pocket calculators are already well understood and we do not gain much if we subject them to AI impact assessments. If we adopt overly narrow definitions, however, and focus only on human-like systems, we may miss significant risks. Current-state autonomous computer systems pose novel problems even if their functionalities are not yet as general as humans'. The fact that humans can be deceived by machines is one important problem, but not the only issue or perhaps even one of the most pressing concerns.

For legal compliance purposes, we need to apply a definition that focuses on the very aspects that require AI to be treated differently from other systems. With laws, we assign legal consequences to human actions and omissions in the interest of societal goals. For example, humans are entitled to copyright protection if they create an original work and are liable for infringement if they reproduce another author's work without a license, because we want to incentivize humans to create original works to benefit the public. When a human uses a deterministic system to create a work or infringe rights, courts can determine authorship and infringement liability relatively easily, based on well-established principles. When AI is involved, however, courts will have to decide *de novo* whether the developer, provider, or user deserves copyrights for computer-generated works or liability for infringements. The key difficulty that judges face is the problem that humans do not fully understand how exactly the AI functions and whether a particular output was caused more by the developer, a provider, or a user. Developers cannot fully predict or control the AI's inner workings or output. As a consequence, we also cannot predict, explain, or prevent malfunctions by AI that could harm humans and violate laws. This is particularly relevant from a legal perspective.

Increased autonomy can – but does not have to – correspond to a loss of control for humans. Engineers have striven for centuries to increase the autonomy of machines in the interest of efficiency, *i.e.*, building systems that need fewer instructions and direction from humans. The less input the user has to provide, the more value the machine adds, for example, a washing machine that can automatically complete cycles of soaking, spinning, and rinsing, or a security camera with a motion sensor that automatically takes and transmits images of intruders. Engineers have not typically tried to build machines that are fully autonomous – meaning self-governing, self-directing, and independent of control – because humans want to limit the machines to carrying out certain objectives. So long as humans retain the ability to define objectives and control machines, substantial machine autonomy by itself does not have to present a significant legal problem.

Traditionally, developers programmed machines to execute a series of predetermined steps. Programmers determine some steps in advance, in the form of software algorithms that instruct the machine to do X when Y happens, defining a path from input to output. Machine operators determine other steps when they use the machine, for example, when they use a pocket calculator or drive a low-tech car. In many modern machines, central processing units (CPUs) execute commands contained in software programs that human programmers have created to pursue pre-determined objectives. For example, when we turn on our laptops in the morning, the computer loads certain applications in which we can view emails and create text documents. The hardware designers, software programmers, and operators of a deterministic system determine numerous steps in the process and the user can predict, understand, and control the effects of the user's input, for example, when the user is typing an email or drafting a document. The fact that programmers can include a randomizer, *i.e.*, software that can produce random numbers to select photos for a screen saver, does not materially change the deterministic character of a system for practical legal purposes, because a human developer made a conscious choice in this regard and can be held responsible, accordingly.

To increase autonomy of deterministic systems, developers have to anticipate and address more and more scenarios to determine how the machine should respond in each situation. Because developers predetermine every step, they can predict, explain, and control the functioning and output of the systems. If a deterministically programmed system does not produce the output that the developer desired for a particular scenario, this indicates either a programming error that the developer could find and correct, or a user error that the operator can avoid. To increase the autonomy of deterministic systems, developers have to contemplate and address myriad potential scenarios and exponentially increase the volumes of instructions expressed in software code to determine the system's output in every conceivable situation. With such deterministic programming approaches, developers reach practical limits of complexity.

More recently, developers have made significant progress in increasing machine autonomy and performance with machine learning techniques. They have created computer systems that do not only follow precise steps programmed with software algorithms, but rather acquire problem-solving capabilities by processing high-level instructions from humans, large data sets, and human feedback applied with supervised and reinforced learning methods. For example, developers have engineered large multi-layer artificial neural networks, modeled after hierarchically organized neurons in human brains, instructed the systems to recognize cats in images, provided numerous images, and then confirmed or corrected the system's identification of images containing cats, continually improving the system's output. In this process, the developers do not instruct the system how to recognize cats – for example, based on size, fur, color, or the number of eyes, ears, and legs – but leave it to the system to identify images depicting cats that a human would associate with a cat, including cartoon images and partial depictions. With reinforcement learning methods, developers simulate rewards for correct output and punishments for incorrect output, without explaining causal connections or programming step-by-step rules on how to recognize cats. Based on the rewards and punishments, the AI adjusts weights in its model representing probabilities relating to patterns and produces increasingly accurate output that the developer did not predetermine with step-by-step programming. Thus, the developer achieves increased system autonomy without having to program individual execution paths to address all inputs. This comes, however, at the cost of reduced control, predictability, and explainability for the human developer and user of the system.

Similarly, companies have created Large Language Models (LLMs) by providing large amounts of text, instructions, and feedback applied with supervised and reinforcement learning techniques to produce text in response to prompts from human users. Developers characterize LLMs also as "generative artificial intelligence (AI)," because the systems are capable of generating text, images, or other media based on probability models derived from patterns and structure of training data that is reflected in output that the LLM generates with similar characteristics. Developers do not instruct LLMs how to answer particular questions based on facts they know or to solve math problems based on algorithms. Instead, the LLMs produce draft text by computing the most probable results based on previous words – similar to how a sophisticated auto-complete feature suggests the next words in a messaging app. An LLM does not normally contain or continuously have access to the data it was trained on. It contains only numeric representations of probabilities in the form of weights, based on which the LLM selects symbols and words to create text or programming code.

Many users – including the author of this Field Guide – are amazed and awed by the usefulness of the LLMs. For example, ChatGPT can pass the California Bar Exam, which a high percentage of students fail after taking three years of law school and tailored bar prep courses. At the same time, users must also acknowledge that LLMs do not apply algorithms to solve math problems or apply scientific methods to answer other questions, and as a result, LLMs can generate inaccurate answers. Developers cannot predict, explain, or control AI output. Users must accept that AI output based on probabilistic methods is only probably correct. This means that probably, it is sometimes incorrect. Users must therefore take responsibility for verifying and correcting or supplementing output before relying on it or disseminating it as fact.

It is this associated loss of predictability, explainability, and control for us humans that poses novel problems. It is also why we should treat AI differently, legally, from deterministic systems. Therefore, in this Field Guide, I propose a definition of AI that focuses specifically on the substantial autonomy of systems and the fact that humans cannot predict, explain, or control the output with certainty.

Even with this focused definition, however, it can be difficult to assess which systems meet the definitional elements. That is where this Field Guide comes in. In the field, you can use several shortcuts and practical methods to identify AI as a species. As a starting point, you can consider what developers and providers call a system. If external suppliers market a system as AI, you should treat it as such until you are able to confirm that it is deterministically programmed. With respect to AI development projects within your organization, you can ask developers to certify whether they can predict, explain, and control the output of a particular system. If you follow recommendations in this Field Guide and designate a human system steward for every relevant system, you can ask the steward to certify whether the system delivers predictable, explainable, and controllable output. If a competent and trustworthy systems steward answers this question in the affirmative, you could reasonably decide to proceed without an impact assessment focused on AI-specific risks, until incidents force you to reconsider the issue. Based on the definition of AI proposed in this Field Guide, it is possible that systems will have to be reclassified over time, because humans will understand and therefore predict and control systems better, as AI research progresses. AI itself can be a great help in this regard if it explains how it generated a certain output, names its sources, and suggests methods how humans can control it (the AI).

Companies also have to monitor the quality and performance of deterministically programmed systems, and developers cannot be expected to certify that any software will ever operate without errors or malfunctions. But, unless and until legislation requires it, companies need not assess every computer program and system for AI-specific risks. If companies conduct too many impact assessments, it will not only hamper their ability to innovate and develop product, but it will also overwhelm their legal and compliance departments. A potential consequence could be that in the flood of paperwork, reviewers miss a truly problematic system that they could have identified and stopped with a more focused approach.

When specific laws and regulations require it, companies will have to apply different definitions of "AI." For example, the EU Parliament proposed in June 2023 the following definition for the EU AI Act:

> "artificial intelligence system" (AI system) means a machine-based system that is designed to operate with varying levels of autonomy and that can, for explicit or implicit objectives, generate outputs such as predictions, recommendations, or decisions, that influence physical or virtual environments.

The EU Commission had previously proposed a definition incorporating an Annex, as follows:

> "artificial intelligence system" (AI system) means software that is developed with one or more of the techniques and approaches listed in Annex I and can, for a given set of human-defined objectives, generate outputs such as content, predictions, recommendations, or decisions influencing the environments they interact with.

At the end of August 2023, the California Privacy Protection Agency (CPPA) published excerpts of draft Risk Assessment Regulations under the California Consumer Privacy Act (CCPA) with a definition according to which

> "Artificial Intelligence" means an engineered or machine-based system that is designed to operate with varying levels of autonomy and that can, for explicit or implicit objectives, generate outputs such as predictions, recommendations, or decisions that influence physical or virtual environments. Artificial intelligence includes generative models, such as large language models, that can learn from inputs and create new outputs, such as text, images, audio, or video; and facial or speech recognition or detection technology.

For purposes of aligning U.S. agencies on AI research, development, and use, the U.S. government enacted the National AI Initiative Act of 2020 according to which

> "artificial intelligence" means a machine-based system that can, for a given set of human-defined objectives, make predictions, recommendations or decisions influencing real or virtual environments. Artificial intelligence systems use machine and human-based inputs to— (A) perceive real and virtual environments; (B) abstract such perceptions into models through analysis in an automated manner; and (C) use model inference to formulate options for information or action.

The National Institute of Standards and Technology (NIST) proposed understanding AI as an

> interdisciplinary field, usually regarded as a branch of computer science, dealing with models and systems for the performance of functions generally associated with human intelligence, such as reasoning and learning.

Companies will have to comply with laws based on such broader definitions if and when they become subject to them. In the meantime, practitioners may find the narrower definition proposed in this Field Guide more effective, because it focusses on the legally crucial aspect of reduced predictability, explainability, and control: "Artificial Intelligence (AI) means computer systems that generate text, images, solutions to problems, and other output, functioning with substantial autonomy and in ways that their developers cannot predict, explain, or control with certainty."

The Territory

Providers in any country can make their AI available in markets worldwide via the World Wide Web. Country borders and local cultures present few obstacles, given the advances in natural language processing developers have achieved. Lawmakers, however, work for nation states. They enact laws and regulations with direct impacts on persons and companies domiciled within their borders, but they have limited powers to enforce their laws in other countries. Therefore, entrepreneurs should carefully consider where they incorporate companies, hire employees, place servers, and establish operations, given that different countries have taken different approaches to regulating AI.

The EU is furthest ahead in restricting AI development and use. The EU has already restricted most forms of data processing by passing the General Data Protection Regulation (GDPR), and it has published a draft new EU AI Act that would impose further prohibitions. Companies in the EU have generally found it difficult to contribute to innovation in the information technology sector and will probably also not be able to advance AI development on EU territory. Given the relative openness of the EU to the Internet and markets, however, individuals and companies in the EU may be able to use AI offered by companies outside the EU, as they have been using other information technologies made in the United States and other countries. If EU data protection authorities keep imposing fines on foreign technology companies, however, it is possible that some will stop offering AI-related services in the EU, as some multinationals have already announced. Yet, the EU Common Market is strategically important to businesses around the world. And as more countries are adopting restrictions similar to the GDPR's on personal data processing, the GDPR may become less of a deterrent for companies offering AI to users in the EU.

Japan amended Article 30 of its Copyright Act in 2019 to allow reproduction of copyrighted works for data extraction and technology development purposes, seemingly to create a better legal environment for machine learning. Japan's data protection authority, however, has issued warnings similar to authorities in the EU with whom Japan agreed on mutual adequacy findings concerning data processing regulations in the context of a trade deal in 2018.

The People's Republic of China (PRC) has been encouraging and supporting public and private-sector entities to pursue AI development for national security applications and other national objectives for decades. But, the PRC also restricts private-sector AI offerings on security policy grounds. The fact that developers cannot predict, explain, or control AI output poses a fundamental obstacle to releasing AI chatbots in the PRC. For example, AI may generate statements that criticize the Chinese Communist Party or conflict with the Chinese government's position. Because the PRC has controlled access to content on the Internet in the PRC since the beginning of the World Wide Web, PRC authorities can block offerings from domestic and foreign companies much more effectively than most other countries. The PRC generally prohibits foreign-owned companies established in China from offering any content or services over the Internet. Also, the PRC blocks AI services offered by foreign companies to users in the PRC.

In the United States, legislatures take a risk-of-harm-based approach to AI regulation, as they have historically taken with respect to privacy protection. California and New York City, for example, have enacted narrowly focused statutes addressing specific concerns pertaining to particular aspects of AI, prohibiting companies from deceiving consumers about the deployment of artificial chatbots and requiring employers to document annual bias audits for automated employment decision tools

("AEDT"). Many other narrowly focused bills in state and federal legislatures are pending and may add up to a patchwork of sector-, harm-,
and situation-specific AI laws resembling the thicket of overlapping and
inconsistent U.S. privacy laws at the federal and state level. At the same
time, class action plaintiffs have launched an avalanche of lawsuits against
AI providers, testing the applicability of existing laws to new offerings
and challenging U.S. courts to lead the way globally in confronting novel
issues pertaining to AI law.

In the rest of the world, governments are cautiously observing the AI
developments and trying to strike a balance between fears of adverse
impacts and fears of missing out on opportunities. Given the potential for
adversaries to weaponize AI for crime and war, governments feel that they
cannot regulate AI too restrictively, which would cause them to lose the
benefits AI offers. At the same time, they fear the potentially devastating
impact of AI on domestic labor markets and social order and pursue an AI
arms race that is as frightening as the race to acquire ever more destruc-
tive nuclear, chemical, and biological weapons.

AI developers, providers, and users have to navigate regulatory land-
scapes across different countries carefully. They will find some jurisdictions provide more friendly legal environments for their development and
deployment plans than others, just as is the case with other technology
products and business models. With respect to cross-border activities, it
can make a significant difference where companies locate their AI development, operation, and use activities, because intellectual property and
computer interference laws apply territorially. For example, developers
typically apply for patents only in some jurisdictions and have to accept
the fact that their inventions can be freely used where they have not
obtained a patent. Also, rights holders find courts in some jurisdictions
more effective than in others. Developers can reduce their risks associated
with scraping and mining copyrighted materials for data acquisition
if they place developer teams or hire service providers in jurisdictions
that are less litigious and do not require defendants to produce records
in pre-trial discovery. If the final AI product does not contain or need
to access training data, as is the case with many systems, companies can
transfer the developed system after the completion of the initial training
phase and thus localize controversial development practices in jurisdictions that explicitly or implicitly allow such practices.

With respect to regulatory restrictions more generally, aside from AI laws
specifically, multinational businesses find many fewer similarities and

much less harmonization than with respect to intellectual property laws. In the United States, a rule of thumb is that everything is allowed if it is not prohibited. Individuals and corporations can develop and deploy new technologies and systems, including AI, except as prohibited by statutes or regulations. Businesses that cause harm with novel and unregulated technologies can be sued based on general tort law principles or broad unfair competition laws in class action lawsuits and by regulators. But, most businesses are able to innovate and expand quickly without being hampered by bureaucratic burdens in the early phases of releasing new technologies if they act responsibly and avoid harms. Over time, businesses have to expect that California and other progressive states will pass specific laws intended to address particular potential harms associated with new technologies.

In Germany and other European countries, courts, regulators, and legislatures have generally taken a more cautious stance concerning potential risks of new technologies. In some cases, they have reversed the basic rule that everything is allowed until it is prohibited. This stance creates risks of its own, namely, that innovators feel stifled, exit the region, and leave problems unaddressed that could be addressed with new technologies.

German courts have held, on questionable constitutional grounds, that new, potentially dangerous technologies are prohibited until they are specifically regulated and allowed, subject to restrictions and conditions. For example, in 1990, an administrative court in Hessen, Germany, preliminarily enjoined a company from operating a gene technology plant until such time that the federal parliament enacts a federal statute regulating gene technologies, due to fears that unregulated businesses could create dangerous monsters threatening humanity. In 1993, German courts started enjoining telecommunications companies from erecting mobile phone antennas on similar grounds, demanding that the parliament address potential health effects of "electrosmog." On similar grounds, courts might prohibit AI due to fears of the rise of machines against humanity.

Particularly relevant for AI is that the German state of Hessen enacted the world's first data protection law in 1970 to address potential risks to civil rights and individual privacy resulting from the deployment of computer systems. The law in Hessen served as a model for data protection laws in other European countries and ultimately the current General Data Protection Regulation (GDPR), which applies to most kinds of private and many public sector data processing activities. The basic premise of

European data protection laws is that the processing of personal data is prohibited, except with valid consent from the data subject or based on another statutory exception. More and more jurisdictions outside of Europe have been adopting similarly prohibitive approaches, including Argentina, Brazil, Colombia, Israel, Japan, Korea, New Zealand, and Uruguay, at least on paper.

Even some U.S. states have adopted principles and specific requirements from the GDPR, led by California with the California Consumer Privacy Act. But, under U.S. laws, AI developers can rely on several reasonable exceptions that are lacking in EU data protection laws. For example, an AI developer can use personal information captured by sensors of an autonomous car or scraped from public websites that the business has a reasonable basis to believe was lawfully made available to the general public by the consumer or from widely distributed media.

The Observed

Developers, providers, and users face different opportunities and risks with respect to AI. Each has to understand the others' roles, both to reduce the risk of contributory liability and because most companies may play more than one role with respect to the different systems or even within a particular system.

Developers create and train AI. They write or select the underlying code and choose training data. They test, monitor, and refine AI with reinforcement learning techniques, simulating rewards for desired outputs and penalties for undesirable outputs.

Providers offer users access to AI functionality. With a web of service providers, they operate computer systems that host the underlying code, models, and data. They design security programs, business models, online user accounts, and commercial terms for customers, who remotely access AI through applications on personal computers, mobile phones, cars, robots, or other systems.

Users use AI to generate various outputs, including text or images, and achieve outcomes such as reaching a destination with an autonomous car. Users can be corporations or individuals who direct AI and can thus mitigate or amplify risks of harm caused by AI output. They can defame others with AI-generated images or video. They can trespass by directing an autonomous car to another person's private property. Users are often more directly responsible for harm caused to a particular individual, and they are often more immediately impacted by harmful AI output, than developers and providers.

The Game Wardens

All government agencies, private sector entities, and individuals within organizations face novel legal issues concerning AI, given its wide range of applications, capabilities, and risks, including those summarized in Chapter 4 of this Field Guide. In the EU, data protection authorities have taken the initiative to regulate AI providers based on the consideration that AI also processes personal data, even if this is not the only or perhaps not even a particularly pressing concern. In the United States, the Equal Employment Opportunity Commission (EEOC) took action against employers based on bias concerns, and the Federal Trade Commission (FTC) is conducting investigations to protect consumers and competition. Other regulators around the world are analyzing the effects of AI on matters within their jurisdiction and competence. Additionally, governments confront tough questions regarding their own use of AI for national and domestic security, law enforcement, employee monitoring, and administration.

Within companies, different departments and individuals take the lead on designing and implementing broader AI law compliance programs. Often, data privacy officers or legal counsels have taken the leading role, given their general focus on data processing, but many organizations realize that they need multidisciplinary working groups and diverse governance boards. You can find suggestions in this regard in Chapter 2 of this Field Guide.

1   Artificial intelligence law

Companies have to comply with a wide range of laws concerning business activities. Some of these laws pose specific new challenges and interpretive problems that companies have to address as they develop, provide, or use Artificial Intelligence (AI) because of the substantial autonomy with which the systems operate and the fact that their developers cannot predict, explain, or control their output with certainty. Such laws can be referred to as "AI law" and you will find an overview of these laws in this first chapter of the Field Guide.

1.1   AI-specific laws

In 2018, California added a Section 17941 to its Business & Professions Code according to which no one may use a bot to communicate with a person in California online and intentionally mislead the other person about its artificial identity for commercial purposes or to influence an election. Companies can avoid liability if they disclose their bots, defined as automated online accounts that artificially generate all or substantially all of the actions or posts of that account. Theoretically, companies are required to disclose deterministically programmed bots, too. But, in practice, humans are far more likely to be deceived by AI-powered bots. Therefore, lawyers consider this California law appropriately as one of the first AI-specific laws.

The United States enacted a National AI Initiative Act of 2020 to coordinate programs across federal government agencies to accelerate AI research and application for prosperity and national security; private sector organizations are not directly subject to this law, but may be indirectly affected, as government contractors or suppliers. Individual states followed suit. For example, Connecticut enacted Public Act No. 23–16 concerning artificial intelligence, automated decision-making, and personal data privacy that took effect on July 1, 2023. Under this law, by December 31, 2023 the Connecticut Department of Administrative

Services shall publish an inventory of all systems that employ artificial intelligence and are in use by any state agency, listing the name of the system and vendor, if any; a description of the general capabilities and uses of such system; whether such system was used to independently make, inform, or materially support a conclusion, decision, or judgment; and whether such system underwent an impact assessment prior to implementation.

Since January 1, 2023, New York City requires employers to evaluate automated employment decision tools ("AEDT") to assesses the likelihood of disparate impact and discrimination based on gender, race, or ethnicity. Employers also have to comply with respect to deterministic decision tools. Yet, AI presents much greater challenges and risks in this respect, because – as already noted – developers cannot predict, explain, or control output with certainty. Hence, employers consider this New York City law an early AI-specific law.

Effective August 15, 2023, the People's Republic of China (PRC) issued "Interim Measures for the Management of Generative Artificial Intelligence Services" based on a number of existing laws. In these interim measures, the PRC declares that providers and users of generative AI services must comply with existing laws concerning "generative AI technology," which is defined as "models and relevant technologies that have the ability to generate content such as texts, images, audio, or video."

As of October 2023, however, lawmakers around the world had not yet enacted any new statutes that are called "AI law" and specifically prescribe how individuals, companies, or research organizations should or must develop, provide, or use AI. Leading AI businesses have warned the public about severe risks associated with AI development, including human extinction. CEOs and computer scientists have joined forces to demand that companies pause further deployment, researchers halt development, and governments regulate AI. This is in stark contrast to how industry leaders and researchers have opposed regulation of novel information technologies in the past, and this backdrop may drive a different trajectory for AI regulation.

Parliamentarians around the world are busy announcing plans to draft AI-specific legislation. The Commission of the European Union (EU) proposed an EU AI Act in 2021 of more than 100 pages, and some companies had considered designing their compliance efforts concerning AI based on the draft EU AI Act. However, when the European Parliament proposed more than 700 amendments to the draft EU AI Act in July 2023, practitioners quickly questioned the benefits of complying with the draft legislation, particularly in light of how many definitions and requirements seem still in play and also based on mounting criticism regarding the many problems that the EU AI Act does not address. Some quipped that while the early bird gets the worm, who likes worms? Companies should watch these developments, but not let the political process distract them from the priority objective of complying with existing laws.

1.2   Product safety, torts, and criminal laws

Governments protect citizens from risks of harm to life and health with myriad laws that prohibit intentionally or negligently hurting persons, engaging in enumerated risky activities, and selling or using products that are known or likely to cause harm. Individuals and companies that violate such prohibitions can be enjoined from specific activities and penalized with a variety of sanctions, including imprisonment of individuals, fines, punitive damages, and compensatory damages. When a victim is killed or injured, law enforcement agencies and courts decide whom to hold responsible and what penalties and liabilities attach, based on complex analyses regarding objective causation, duties of conduct, and degrees of subjective fault.

For example, in any traffic accident, drivers, car manufacturers, and various other persons or organizations typically contribute to some degree to a chain of events, including a driver who may have exceeded the speed limit, a passenger who distracted the driver with a question, a car manu-facturer that opted for cheap brake pads, a car owner who failed to keep regular maintenance appointments, a barkeeper who poured too much liquor into a drink for the driver, a dog owner whose animal ran into the street, or a business owner whose bright neon advertisement impaired the driver's vision. Over decades, lawmakers have developed numerous rules concerning individual obligations and responsibilities pertaining to automotive safety features, car maintenance, driving conduct, the sale and consumption of alcohol, animal control, and roadside advertise-ments. Also, courts have developed rules on how to allocate individual responsibility for harms caused by multiple human actors and factors.

The car manufacturer will not typically be held responsible if the brakes performed in accordance with specifications and applicable regulations and there is no design defect. The car owner may face civil liability for damage caused to third parties by the car. In most countries, a car owner is required to obtain mandatory automobile liability insurance to cover property damage and bodily injury to third parties, which ensures that victims of an accident involving the owner's car will get a minimum level of compensation for damages. A barkeeper will typically not be held responsible for an accident caused by a drunk driver, unless the barkeeper induced the driver to drive after drinking or had strong reasons to foresee and prevent the drunk driving. An animal owner faces strict liability for damage caused by the animal but will not normally be prosecuted criminally.

To determine how these rules will apply in situations involving AI, judges may consider analogies and a variety of arguments that lawyers will present and that will be accepted or rejected over time. For example, a person in the driver's seat of an autonomous or semi-autonomous car may not be responsible as a driver. If AI steers a car into a white wall that it cannot distinguish from white clouds on the horizon, the manufacturer may face strict liability instead of, or in addition to, any responsibility borne by the car owner. Perhaps manufacturers should be required to obtain automobile liability insurance, and not car owners anymore, because the relative degree of risk no longer depends as much on the car owner or human driver, but largely on the AI in the car. But, whether a victim can prove that the car manufacturer is responsible for an accident involving numerous contributing factors will require novel analyses. By my definition, no one can predict, explain, or control the functioning of AI with the same degree of certainty that an investigator could find a programming error in deterministic automotive systems or, where a programming error is not found, instead decide that external factors were mostly to blame.

In the absence of new legislation, courts may lean toward holding AI owners strictly liable for physical harm caused to humans and physical property based on similar principles and policy considerations to those they have used to hold car and animal owners strictly liable. A person or company that owns an autonomous car, robot, or other AI and operates it for their own use or to provide services to others, or that lets others operate the AI, should thus prepare to be strictly liable for damages caused by the AI. An AI-driven product owner should consider obtaining insurance for liability caused to third parties or securing indemnification from the AI supplier, as further discussed in Chapter 5 of this Field Guide. Lawmakers may consider mandating basic insurance for more than cars, perhaps requiring AI providers to obtain insurance for products where the individual owner or operator does not contribute materially to the risks emanating from the AI. In 2022, the European Commission published a draft directive on adapting non-contractual civil liability rules to artificial intelligence (AI Liability Directive), which supplements the separate draft EU AI Act and provides for rebuttable presumptions of non-compliance and causal links.

With respect to criminal liability and liability for punitive damages, courts typically mete out penalties to punish the guilty, deter criminals from breaking laws again, deter the public from committing similar offenses, incapacitate criminals (by imprisoning them), and re-socialize convicts. Humans can be influenced by punishment, while AI cannot. Where companies replace humans with AI, criminal laws and punitive liability may prove ineffective, unless courts hold humans criminally accountable for the mere deployment of AI or for harm caused by AI that was insufficiently tested or monitored. In real life examples, AI has already featured in criminal trials. In 2015, the U.S. Department of Justice charged companies and individual defendants with criminal antitrust law violations in a case involving price fixing by algorithms. Where individual employees might have been reluctant to agree on minimum prices with competitors for fear of jail time under antitrust laws, AI quickly aligned prices with AI deployed by competitors in order to optimize returns. Companies have to expect that prosecutors will try to hold individual executives, developers, or operators responsible for failure to prevent price fixing or other harms committed by AI and plan their corporate compliance measures accordingly.

Companies should conduct AI risk assessments to identify potential harms and risk mitigation measures with the primary goal of preventing harm and the secondary goal of creating defenses against charges and claims of liability. Just as a company can reduce the risk of liability for actions and omissions by rogue employees, companies can reduce risks emanating from AI if they implement robust compliance programs, as proposed in Chapters 2 and 3 of this Field Guide. If companies identify and mitigate knowable risks, they can better defend themselves against charges of causation and individual culpability. Based on risk assessments proposed in Chapter 4 of this Field Guide, companies can apply guardrails to reduce the risk of certain harms. Also, companies can warn AI users and third parties to prevent risky AI use or at a minimum shift responsibility of risky AI use from developers and providers to AI users, as proposed in Chapters 5 and 6 of this Field Guide.

1.3   Property laws

In most societies and legal systems, individuals can own land, animals, tangible goods, and intellectual property. Governments allocate property rights to individuals to encourage behaviors that benefit the public. For example, a farmer is more likely to invest time and resources into planting and raising animals if the farmer can assert real property law to exclude others from entering to harvest the fruits of the farmer's labor. Manufacturers and dealers are more motivated to invest in the making and distributing of tools and other products if they can exclude others from duplicating the products and their branding and selling those duplicates. Authors and inventors invest in creation and inventions if they can exclude others from copying their works or using their inventions without compensation. The public benefits from the availability of food, products, creative works, and inventions. Workers are freed up for specialization and economic development through division of labor. With myriad rules and exceptions, lawmakers carefully balance public access interests and individual exclusion rights to ensure that property owners do not use their exclusion rights to the unreasonable detriment of others, *e.g.*, by limiting property rights through:

- eminent domain, allowing the state to expropriate land, subject to paying compensation, in order to build roads, railways, dams, and other public works;
- rights of way and access for adjacent landowners;
- exhaustion principles (*a.k.a.* "first sale doctrine") allowing buyers to resell lawful copies of works, trademarked goods, or patented products in the interest of commerce and competition;
- fair use defenses, allowing the public to reproduce copyrighted works for purposes of creating new, transformative works if this does not unduly affect the market for the copied works; and

- mandatory licensing schemes, *e.g.*, to secure affordable drugs to prevent public health crises.

Legislatures, courts, and practicing lawyers have to reconsider these balancing decisions in cases involving AI. Because of the substantial autonomy in which AI operates and the fact that its developer cannot predict, explain, or control AI functionality or output with certainty, a lawmaker or judge can find it difficult to determine whether AI output constitutes an infringing copy of material that developers used to train the AI, a derivative work that can be defended based on fair use principles, a licensed derivative work created based on user input, or a new original work based on the developer's or user's creativity. Open source code programmers, writers, artists, comedians, and other creators as well as online service platform operators have brought numerous lawsuits against AI developers for scraping data and content without authorization and infringing property rights to train AI that is increasingly capable of replacing creators and competing with online services. Therefore, companies have to carefully consider property rights and infringement risks in the context of developing, providing, and using AI.

1.3.1   Ownership of AI, input, and output

As with any other technologies, developers of AI can acquire copyrights, patents, and other intellectual property rights to original or novel systems. But, they do not typically acquire property rights to output that systems generate, unless they can show that the human developers themselves invented or authored the output. Typically, the human developer cannot claim invention or authorship to output of AI, because of the autonomy and unpredictability of the systems. By contrast, with respect to deterministically programmed systems, developers can prove a closer connection to the system's output than with respect to AI, because the developer can predict, explain, and control the output.

Some output is too functional or utilitarian to qualify for copyright and not novel or nonobvious enough to qualify for patent protection. For example, the developer of a deterministic calculator pre-determines the number that a calculator provides in response to a prompt, but this number cannot qualify for copyright protection because it is dictated by mathematics. Developers of video games, on the other hand, create artwork for characters and backgrounds that constitute copyrightable output. With respect to word processing software programs, developers include some predetermined, creative elements in user interfaces that the systems produce on user screens subject to the developer's copyrights. But, developers or word processing software programs leave it completely up to users to create text aided by the software, thus not creating any basis for a claim by the developer that it has any copyrights in user-generated output. With respect to deterministic systems, output can typically be explained either by actions of the developer or user, which makes the allocation of copyrights to output relatively easy.

Users of AI can own copyrights to creative input and possibly patents to inventions on which they base novel prompts or other input submitted to the AI system. But, like developers of AI systems, users of AI systems can also not typically acquire copyrights or patents to the AI system's output. The amount of creativity or inventive innovation that a user may invest in engineering prompts or may otherwise include in input will typically appear minimal compared to the amount of valuable information and problem-solving advances in AI output. Moreover, a user of AI cannot predict, explain, or control output in a comparable manner to how a user can predict, explain, or control output of a deterministic system, for example, output in the form of a text that a user writes with a word processing document. In most cases, therefore, one has to assume that the output of AI systems cannot qualify for copyrights, patents, or other intellectual property rights protection.

Courts will likely find it quite compatible with the legislative purpose of intellectual property laws that output of AI does not typically qualify for intellectual property protection, because lawmakers have granted such rights only for the purpose of encouraging humans to innovate in the public interest. Courts and the copyright and patent offices in the U.S. have already denied copyright protection with respect to photos created by a monkey operating a camera and applications for copyrights and patents for works and inventions generated by AI. Under constitutions and intellectual property law statutes, human innovators are rewarded with patents, copyrights, and other intellectual property rights where they conceive inventions and create artistic works. The intellectual property rights owners can monetize their innovations by charging others license fees for using or selling their inventions or making copies of their works, or by excluding others from the marketplace and themselves charging higher prices for copies and products. Lawmakers grant such incentives to encourage innovation and progress in the public interest, just as landowners are encouraged with real property rights to develop or farm their land and owners of chattels are encouraged with property rights to make tools and other useful products. For this purpose, developers of AI receive intellectual property rights in the development of AI.

But, once the developer has created AI, there is no equally compelling need to incentivize providers or users of AI to generate AI output. Machines do not need or benefit from legal incentives. Providers operating AI do not innovate much, when AI generates output. Providers mostly keep the systems powered, connected, and secure. Users may invest some creative energy when they engineer innovative prompts, but their contribution to AI-generated output is often relatively minor. Therefore, users may not be viewed as the ones primarily responsible for innovation when AI generates output. Accordingly, lawmakers may not see a need to change intellectual property laws to grant property rights in output generated by AI. They may find it sufficient that the developers of AI are rewarded with property rights in the systems they create.

1.3.2   Infringement

Developers and users of AI can infringe intellectual property rights of others when they create and use AI. For example, when developers copy text, images, and other works from websites to create training data sets for machine learning, they infringe copyrights unless they obtain a license or benefit from a statutory defense. Also, users can infringe intellectual property rights if they prompt AI to create output that is likely to infringe based on the nature of the prompt, *e.g.*, by submitting a copyrighted text and asking for a translation, or by requesting a poem or painting in the style of a living author and resembling a particular work. Providers can be contributorily or vicariously liable for infringements caused by users. Developers and providers may also be liable for copyright infringement when AI produces output that resembles materials contained in data sets that developers inserted into the AI during the training phase.

Plaintiffs can successfully bring copyright claims where output is partially identical or similar to copyrighted works if they can show that the defendant had access to such works, which plaintiffs can do with relative ease with respect to open source code and widely published works. AI developers may find it difficult to defend against such claims, because they cannot point to their own human creativity to explain the origins of

AI output or provide alternative explanations why AI output resembles a copyrighted work, given that they can generally not predict, explain, or control AI functionality or output.

AI developers may try to assert the fair use defense under U.S. copyright law and similar theories under laws in other jurisdictions. Under such theories, creators are permitted to reproduce and adapt excerpts of copyrighted works without a license for public benefit purposes such as news reporting, teaching, and research. Courts in the U.S. have also permitted defendants to rely on the fair use doctrine where the defendant created a new transformative work that did not harm the market for the reproduced work. But, courts may not classify AI-generated output as transformative, because it lacks the human-generated creativity that copyright law is intended to encourage. Courts may consider that the AI output is not a highly creative and innovative work if they liken it to a sophisticated photocopy machine. Artists have publicly complained that AI output is used instead of their works and thus harms market prospects for their works. This, and the fact that many AI developers, providers, and users operate for profit and that developers reproduce entire works for machine learning purposes may mean that they cannot rely on the fair use doctrine and must obtain licenses before they use copyrighted material for AI development. Perhaps in light of this current limitation based on intellectual property law, Japan amended Article 30 of its Copyright Act in 2019 to allow reproduction of copyrighted works for data extraction and technology development purposes, seemingly to create a better legal environment for machine learning.

1.3.3   Open source license terms

Companies find that open source code presents a key source of opportunities and compliance risks, because it is widely available and comes with restrictions that are easy to overlook. When developers look for training data, open source code is more easily accessible than most code and other content. Most software companies keep their proprietary software internal these days and, as a service, offer its functionality via limited remote access over the Internet. AI developers cannot access such code, except with express permission. Companies that still distribute software on disks or devices usually ship only object code, composed of digitized zeros and ones, which cannot be read by humans and may also be less useful for AI training. But, developers can easily find vast amounts of open source code on Github, Gitlab, and a variety of other repositories, portals, and websites, free of charge and for anyone to use.

In open source code license terms, copyright owners allow anyone to copy, adapt, or distribute their works and apply only a few restrictions. Typically, open source code licensors require that users acknowledge authorship and pass on the license terms with copies or derivative works. Also, under the General Public License (GPL) and a few other free source code licenses, licensees have to make any of their derivative works also available in source code form, under the same license terms, to keep the code accessible and free. Programmers thoughtfully invented free source code license models to counteract what they perceived as adverse impacts of copyright law on software development. Ever since courts first decided to afford copyright protection to computer programs decades ago, companies had a strong incentive to avoid reusing existing code owned by others, which could subject them to license fee payment obligations. Because independent creation is a defense to copyright infringement, software development companies often opted for creating programs from scratch, ideally in a "clean room" environment, so they could prove that their products were not copies of existing programs with similar functionality. Programmers did not appreciate the impact that this dynamic had on their professional lives and day-to-day assignments: instead of being asked to further develop and improve the "state of the art" and to focus on cutting-edge problems, programmers were asked to spend most of their time reinventing the wheel.

To reverse these negative consequences of copyrights, programmers propagated "copyleft" and designed open source code license terms to free software from the shackles and chains of copyright protection. The Free Software Foundation promoted the spread of "freed software," licensed under the GPL, to replace and ultimately eliminate proprietary software commercialized through restrictive licensing. Fighting fire with fire, they pursued this goal with enforcement mechanisms under copyright law: any copyright owner who released software under the GPL would require anybody else to apply the GPL to any new versions of that code and could bring copyright infringement actions against anyone who breached the GPL. Anybody who distributed software outside the scope of the applicable license agreements lacked a valid authorization required by copyright law and thus committed copyright infringement. Most programmers supported this approach, donated time and code to projects, proposed additional open source code license terms, and advocated for open source code usage at their employers. Companies found ways to adjust their business models and benefited from productivity increases.

A number of AI developers and providers have been sued by plaintiffs asserting that AI output infringes copyrights, because it contains or constitutes copies of open source code and the applicable open source code license terms are not complied with. In a copyright lawsuit, a plaintiff has to show that the allegedly infringing work is similar to the infringed work, that the plaintiffs own copyrights to the infringed work, and that the defendant had access to the infringed work. Myriad contributors own copyrights to open source code that AI developers have access to. AI developers, providers, and users face a particular difficulty in defending against such lawsuits due to the fact that developers cannot predict, explain, or control output with certainty, making it hard to explain the similarity of output based on non-infringing factors (*e.g.*, that functional necessities, not human creativity, dictated certain elements of code). Also, AI developers and users may not be able to rely on the fair use defense, because they cannot point to transformative human creativity in the generation of AI output. Courts may dismiss arguments that the creativity in the AI development itself counts as creativity in output on the same grounds that courts would not agree that copying with photocopy machines is creative because the code in the photocopy machine is creative.

AI users can screen output for potential infringements, *e.g.*, by using software tools by Black Duck, Gitlab, or Github that identify published open course code elements in programs. Once an AI user has determined which open source license terms apply to existing code that resembles the AI output, the user could comply with such license terms. In some cases, AI users may find that several open source license terms may potentially be implicated and that such terms are not compatible with one another. Yet, most open source code contributors will appreciate a reasonable effort to comply and be appeased by a good faith effort to play by open source rules. Thus, AI users should be able to significantly reduce the risk of infringement claims by owners of copyrights in existing open source code, even if they are not able to determine and comply with all requirements 100 percent.

Another question that AI developers have to consider with respect to openness is whether they should publish not only the underlying code but also the weights and machine learning techniques they used to create AI. In addition to economic and competitive considerations, some cite safety and security concerns against opening up AI. They point to the many dangerous use cases that criminals, terrorist groups, and rogue nation states could pursue with AI as well as risks associated with unintended consequences of poorly configured or deployed AI, many of which are discussed in Chapter 4 of this Field Guide. Others believe that greater openness will enable the well-intentioned majority of humans and nations to protect humanity more efficiently from threats posed by a few bad actors. Some organizations propose striking a balance by releasing older versions of AI under open terms while keeping details regarding the most advanced versions closed and secret.

1.3.4   Computer interference and trespass

Developers use web crawlers, bots, and "scraping" technologies to automatically access websites to copy content for different business purposes, including to support search engines and to gather training data for machine learning purposes. With such methods, developers can violate copyrights, trespass laws, and the United States Computer Fraud and Abuse Act (CFAA), unless the owners of the scraped websites expressly or impliedly authorize automated access and downloads in their website terms of use. The Wikimedia Foundation, for example, generously allows scraping and reproduction of Wikipedia content. Other site operators expressly prohibit scraping, because their business models rely on human visitors. Many companies neither prohibit nor allow scraping.

Companies have been scraping so commonly that the Practising Law Institute (PLI) hosted a conference in 2014 with the title, "Everyone's Doing It, But Is It Legal? Web Scraping and Online Data Harvesting." Many online companies scrape content off other sites while complaining about being victims of scraping themselves. They use automated software scripts that harvest text, images, and other data from websites, often for commercial purposes. Most companies welcome the robots deployed by search engines to ensure their websites are easily found. At the same time, however, they typically try to protect their sites from scraping and deep-linking that causes users to bypass portal sites (and their advertisements) or that otherwise affects their business interests adversely.

For example, operators of classified advertising websites, e-commerce marketplaces, real estate listing aggregators, and social media companies have sued competitors and their service providers, based on the U.S. Computer Fraud and Abuse Act (CFAA) and similar laws, for harvesting and reproducing content from their sites. In most cases, the plaintiffs won if they were able to show that they clearly prohibit scraping in their website terms of use and apply technical measures against automated access and copying, including robot.txt notices in metadata, account registration requirements, and CAPTCHAs to keep away robots. In some cases, courts required plaintiffs to issue specific warnings before filing a lawsuit, and companies now issue such warnings routinely where they can identify the operator of the unwanted scraping.

In 2017, a court in California enjoined a prominent social media company from excluding a company that scraped personal data of social media site users without the social media company's authorization or any compensation for the data, based on the court's perception regarding the balance of hardships and public interests in the availability of data. After many appeals, the social media company seems to be gaining the upper hand in the ongoing dispute, but the diverging court decisions in this high-profile litigation campaign have also emboldened many AI developers who may have figured it is easier to ask for forgiveness than for permission. In 2023, U.S.-based law firms representing class action plaintiffs have unleashed an avalanche of lawsuits against prominent AI developers based on CFAA and trespass laws. Large publishers and social media companies have announced that they expect to be paid for data access going forward. AI developers should therefore implement reasonable procedures to avoid violating other companies' website terms of use and circumventing technological barriers to access computers without permission.

At the same time, companies should consider how they position themselves in favor of or against scraping of their own websites. They should consider updating their website terms of use, implementing technological barriers to scraping, and adopting potential licensing programs. If companies decide they want to charge for data, they have to consider data rights more holistically.

1.3.5   Data rights

AI developers do not have to be as concerned about property rights concerning data as they should be concerning copyrights and computers. No one owns data. Particularly, data subjects do not own data concerning themselves in a property law sense. In most jurisdictions, to safeguard freedom of information and speech, facts and information are generally carved out and not subject to property rights even though businesses find data extremely valuable.

To some extent, companies can use unfair competition and copyright-like property law regimes to protect their investment in databases against wholesale, literal copying and use. The creator of a database owns limited property rights in the database under laws in the EU and other jurisdictions outside the United States. Under U.S. law, database owners can assert unfair competition laws and state law theories against misappropriation, but federal courts often deny protection based on preemption arguments under Section 102(b) of the U.S. Copyright Act, which provides that copyright protection does not extend to ideas, procedures, processes, systems, methods of operation, concepts, principles, or discoveries and is generally understood also to exclude mere factual data. AI developers should therefore be careful to respect database owners' rights.

Aside from that, data brokers and AI developers have to carefully consider rights to data and whether they should compensate their data suppliers. Website operators obtain data from a variety of sources, including employees, independent contractors, corporate service providers, and data brokers, but also from individual creators who post user-generated content and consumers who provide personal information when they use a site. Under the California Consumer Privacy Act (CCPA), businesses that offer a financial incentive to consumers (*e.g.*, a loyalty program or a free online service) when they collect personal information have to disclose the value of personal information in a Notice of Financial Incentives, and offer rights to opt out of the selling of personal information. In both California and Vermont, data brokers that buy and resell personal information have to register with authorities and comply with particular disclosure requirements. Companies that buy personal information from brokers have to consider whether their contemplated use of the personal information is reasonably necessary and proportionate to achieve the purposes for which the personal information was originally collected, or they have to ensure that the broker has obtained informed consent for a new data use, including AI development. If a company pays some data suppliers yet scrapes data off of other sites without authorization or compensation, a plaintiff may refer to payments for data in order to substantiate damages claims in connection with lawsuits against scraping.

1.4   Trade secrets, confidentiality, and security

Under trade secret laws, businesses can protect know-how, customer lists, and other confidential information from unfair misappropriation by competitors if they keep the information secret with reasonable measures and derive independent economic value from keeping the information secret. Developers can invoke trade secret protection if they keep their algorithms, code, weights, training data, machine learning, reinforcement training methods, and other know-how confidential. Developers, providers, and users can also protect AI output against misappropriation under trade secret law if they can keep the output secret. In practice, this will be easier with respect to AI that the developers and providers operate under strict confidentiality agreements. If providers offer the public access to AI, neither the provider nor any users can probably claim trade secret protection for output that the AI would give to any other user who submits a similar prompt, because neither the provider nor the users can apply reasonable means to keep the information secret.

AI users have to carefully consider whether they should submit confidential information to AI provided by third parties. If the AI captures insights from the input via machine learning dynamics, other users may gain access to the information and it may cease to qualify as a trade secret. For example, if automakers use AI to design new cars and submit novel designs or materials information in the process, the AI may include information on such details in responses to user prompts of competing manufacturers that may be using the same AI as part of benchmarking services or insights. Similar concerns apply in principle where manufacturers outsource research and development to human consultants who learn on the job, but consulting firms have been able to address concerns through staff training, non-disclosure agreements, and non-compete covenants. AI users may be more concerned with respect to AI, because developers cannot predict, explain, or control AI output as well as consultancy firms are expected to manage confidentiality by their employees.

You can find data security requirements not only in trade secret laws and policies or confidentiality agreements, but also in privacy laws and data processing regulations such as the GDPR, discussed in more detail in Section 1.8 of this chapter. You should consider a holistic approach to address all security requirements, because their common objective is to prevent unauthorized access to information. Many measures that a company can deploy to pursue this objective are or should be identical. Therefore, companies should combine and leverage technical security measures to protect trade secrets, confidential information, and personal data from security threats – instead of running separate, disparate programs, managed by different teams, in different silos, within the same company. For example, companies should not just adopt "cybersecurity" measures to address threats of online attacks. Rather, companies should adopt measures that both repel attacks and keep their premises secure and address insider threats, including risks that employees or service providers may disseminate confidential information, maliciously or by mistake.

At the same time, companies should keep in mind differences in laws when they draft contracts and design administrative and organizational privacy, trade secret, and data protection measures. Under U.S. privacy laws, companies have to respect reasonable privacy expectations of individuals and comply with specifically prescribed restrictions and requirements. But, publicly available information that does not affect reasonable privacy expectations is often carved out. Businesses can protect any valuable information as a trade secret if they apply reasonable means of security, but protection ends once the secret is disseminated. European-style data processing regulations apply even to personal data that has become public. Therefore, attorneys need to differentiate between the different regimes in contracts. Companies cannot agree to typical definitional carve-outs in confidentiality clauses concerning independently developed information, information in the public domain, or compelled disclosures with respect to personal data that is subject to European-style data processing regulations. Companies have to confirm compliance with data protection law requirements separately and in addition to compliance with trade secret laws and contractual confidentiality obligations.

In the past, most laws and contract clauses simply set forth a general reasonableness standard, and contracting parties did not have to prescribe specific safeguards. This changed, however, after California enacted the world's first data security breach notification law in 2002; other jurisdictions followed, and companies around the world started reporting security breaches en masse. Since then, companies and lawmakers have started prescribing very specific technical, administrative, and organizational data security measures (TOMs) to ensure that companies make more effective efforts to prevent security breaches and protect the data and privacy of consumers, employees, and other individuals. Most companies find such measures equally helpful or necessary for the protection of confidential information and trade secrets.

1.5   Anti-discrimination

Developers of credit scoring or job application screening software can avoid violating anti-discrimination laws relatively easily by programming deterministic systems to disregard race, gender, and other categories of information that system users must not base credit or hiring decisions on. Even with respect to deterministic systems and human decision-making, companies find it challenging to ensure they also consider and appropriately disregard indirect factors, such as names or languages, as indicators of ethnic backgrounds. But, with sufficient planning and training, companies can reduce risks of unlawful bias to a legally acceptable level.

With respect to AI, however, a fundamental problem lies in the substantial autonomy with which the systems operate and the fact that their developers cannot predict, explain, or control their functionality or output with certainty. If a minority applicant challenges you with respect to a rejection of a loan or job application based on AI-generated processes, and proves that the AI rejects a relatively higher number of minority applications than human decision-makers or deterministic systems, the AI user cannot easily prove that the decision was not directly or indirectly influenced by unlawful bias, because it cannot explain the AI output with certainty. In a recent case, the U.S. Equal Employment Opportunity Commission (EEOC) fined a foreign employer for the deployment of AI that discriminated against older candidates. Applicants complained to the EEOC after their applications with their true age were rejected, but accepted after they submitted an application with identical information except for a younger age.

Even without such compelling evidence, courts may hold it against the AI user that the AI may have generated its decision based on probabilistic methods and statistical correlations between loan defaults and race, age, or gender – defaults that were caused by the very historic discrimination practices that governments seek to overcome by prohibiting the consideration of race, gender, or age for credit decisions. To eliminate unconscious and unlawful human bias, employers have to conduct training and instruct employees appropriately with protocols. AI developers can address some risks by carefully selecting training data and training methods, but they will also have to monitor output and verify that the overall outcome of AI-based decision-making does not show statistical indications of discrimination.

1.6   Privacy and defamation

Most humans assert rights to be let alone and not to be slandered mostly against other humans. Few are concerned whether a fly watches them undress or wonder what a seagull thinks of them. With respect to AI, security cameras, or other machines, humans are also typically not concerned with what the machine observes or records, but they are concerned whether other humans could ultimately access the information. If the owner of a nanny-cam leaves a device unintentionally recording, or if a poorly performing voice transcript program writes down erroneous statements, most system owners will typically not feel impaired in their privacy or reputation if they can delete the footage or text before any person sees it.

Similarly, a user of an AI chatbot should not typically feel an intrusion into privacy or reputation rights if AI output contains incorrect or offensive statements concerning the user so long as the user can be sure that no one else sees the same kind of output or, at a minimum, no one considers the output as a true statement. Individuals should be able to feel secure about the lack of privacy impact or reputational harm when AI suggests words or text (based on probabilistic methods) in contexts where other users are unlikely to consider the text factually accurate. For example, users of messaging apps sometimes send unintended messages when they fail to correct text partially produced by the auto-suggest or auto-correct feature of the app. Similarly, human assistants or junior interns may prepare first drafts of legal memos that everyone understands may contain inaccuracies and that should therefore not affect anyone's privacy or reputational rights so long as the drafts are understood as such.

With respect to output of AI chatbots, however, plaintiffs have complained in lawsuits about privacy intrusions or defamation simply on the basis that other users may receive similar output and misunderstand it as a factual statement about them. AI providers should be able to defend against such claims if they can show that they make AI users sufficiently aware that the AI output should be understood to merely constitute draft text generated based on probabilistic methods that users must verify or correct before relying on or disseminating it to others as a statement of fact. If plaintiffs can prove, however, that other users relied on the output as factually accurate, or that they disseminated the output in ways that affected the plaintiff's privacy or reputation, courts may hold the users liable, and potentially also the AI provider and developer, based on theories of contributory or vicarious liability. For example, in 2012, a German plaintiff obtained an injunction against a search engine provider whose auto-complete feature suggested that users who entered her name into a search field add "prostitute" as additional search term. The defendant argued that search engine users should have understood that the auto-complete suggestion only indicated that other users had recently entered such search terms and not that the plaintiff was, knew, or perhaps sued a prostitute, or perhaps opposed prostitution. Nevertheless, a German court issued an injunction against the search engine provider requiring a reconfiguration of the auto-complete suggestion engine that would no longer suggest the offending words in connection with searches using the plaintiff's name.

Where an auto-complete feature is based on deterministic programming, a provider should be able to explain – and a user should be able to understand – why the system made a particular auto-complete suggestion. Users can relatively easily understand that a suggestion does not come with any implied authority if it is based simply on how often the user or other users have used a particular word combination in a search or sentence. Yet, users may not as easily or intuitively understand why AI produces a certain output, particularly given that not even its developers can predict, explain, or control its functionality or output. Therefore, AI developers and providers should conspicuously warn users about inaccuracies and limitations concerning AI output. They should clearly describe accuracy expectations in their terms of use and additionally educate users about the meaning of AI output to reduce the risk of misunderstandings concerning its reliability. Providers should also contractually require AI users to verify the factual accuracy of draft text or decisions that AI produces before the user relies on the output for decision-making or disseminates it to others.

1.7   Publicity

Individuals own a right to prohibit or monetize their name and likeness for commercial purposes. For example, companies need to obtain consent from data subjects before using their pictures in advertisements. AI developers also need to obtain permission from individuals if they want to train AI to imitate a particular person's likeness, *e.g.*, to create audiobooks with celebrity voices or computer-generated movie characters. Where AI developers use images, video, or voice recordings to train AI to imitate human behavior more generally, however, individual rights to publicity may not be implicated if output cannot reasonably be associated with an individual person. AI developers have to carefully test and monitor output in this regard, because they may not be able to explain any coincidental likeness of AI-generated output to the identity to living persons, given that they generally cannot predict, explain, or control AI functionality and output.

1.8   GDPR and other data processing regulations

AI developers, providers, and users that operate in the European Economic Area, Switzerland, or the UK ("EEA+") or other countries that have adopted the EU's General Data Protection Regulation (GDPR) have to justify all processing of personal data. The EU updated and harmonized its data protection laws in 2016 in the form of the GDPR, which is not limited to protecting privacy, but also covers other rights and freedoms of natural persons. In fact, the word "privacy" does not appear even once in the GDPR's lengthy recitals and operative text. Commentators have appropriately called the GDPR "the law of everything." The GDPR prohibits any processing of personal data by default and defines the terms "personal data" and "processing" so broadly that AI developers, providers, and users are covered at least tangentially, even if their applications are not focused on personal data.

1.8.1   Personal data

Personal data means any information relating to an identified or identifiable natural person ("data subject"), for example, an inventor named in a patent application or an unnamed social media user whose post an AI developer includes in a training data set. Also, the user name and access credentials of an individual representative of a corporate AI user, as well as any prompts submitted by this person, qualify as personal data under the GDPR, and the AI provider and user have to treat them as such. Whether information stored within the AI or its output constitutes personal data depends on how the AI provider and user view such information: If they agree that a Large Language Model (LLM) merely drafts text based on probabilistic methods, like a giant auto-suggest or auto-complete engine, then they should understand the LLM more like a dictionary and the output like an auto-generated proposal that the user needs to select or reject before any meaning can be attributed to it. We would not normally consider a dictionary or a rough first draft of an answer prepared by a human assistant who does not know the facts as containing personal data merely because names appear in them. With respect to AI, we need to similarly differentiate at what point output can be considered factual. AI providers and users need to align on this point to allocate responsibilities for accuracy appropriately.

1.8.2   De-identification and synthetic data

Data can cease to qualify as "personal data" if it is redacted or aggregated in a manner that destroys the connection to an individual. Encryption and partial, reversible, or temporary redaction (also known as "pseudonymization") can be legally required and help address security risks. But, they do not render data "anonymous" if someone holds the key and could re-identify the data subject. For the most part, you still have to treat encrypted or pseudonymized data as "personal data" under data protection laws.

With irreversible aggregation, however, developers can remove data from the scope of data protection laws. For example, if you take information on video rental habits of a thousand randomly selected individuals, and you merge the information to create statistical information about a group that contains less than all of the 1,000 individuals, the resulting aggregate data (*e.g.*, 20 percent of video renters watch less than 20 hours a month) is no longer "personal data" (while the raw data on individual habits continues to be personal data). Theoretically, you could also redact data relating to an individual by removing names and all identifiers from a profile. But this is harder to do, in practice, than you might think. If the redacted data sets preserve any information (*e.g.*, an address or birth date) that allows the reversal of the redaction process, then the data will typically continue to qualify as "personal data" under the GDPR. Reversible redaction and other forms of pseudonymization do not remove data from the scope of European data protection laws, but they are recognized as legitimate and potentially required security measures.

As a rule of thumb, AI developers, providers, and users should presume that data is "personal" unless they can positively confirm that particular data does not relate to any identifiable individual. They can try to "anonymize" or "de-identify" personal data and create "synthetic data" to avoid or address restrictions under privacy laws and to mitigate security risks. Companies can satisfy both objectives if they irreversibly remove any link in a data set that can be used to identify an individual person. U.S. health information privacy law, namely the Privacy Rule under HIPAA, for example, specifies identifiers that companies have to remove from protected health information or, alternatively, a process by which companies can engage a statistician to qualify data sets as sufficiently de-identified. Yet, the more information a company removes from a data set, the less valuable the remaining information is for machine learning, research, development, precision medicine, marketing, and various other business purposes.

Companies have to consider that re-identification risks steadily increase with the rise of computing power, big data, and analytics capabilities. In practice, some companies use terms like "anonymous" or "anonymized" loosely for data that qualifies only as "redacted" or "pseudonymized" under the GDPR, CCPA, or other laws. Therefore, AI developers, providers, and users should always carefully examine whether data sets are subject to privacy law restrictions even if they are presented as anonymized.

1.8.3   Publicly available data

Californians adopted many GDPR principles in the California Consumer Privacy Act (CCPA) but, in a 2020 amendment, excluded publicly available information from the definition of "personal information" and thus any restrictions under the CCPA. Developers can be less concerned about CCPA in the context of data acquisition from public websites, because the CCPA does not apply to information that a business has a reasonable basis to believe is lawfully made available to the general public by the consumer or from widely distributed media. India seems to have taken a similar approach in its Digital Personal Data Protection Act enacted on August 11, 2023, exempting publicly available data from its scope and also permitting the processing of personal data necessary for research or statistical purposes. Under the laws of many countries, personal data is not protected if the data subject publishes it intentionally.

But, to the extent the GDPR applies to data processing, developers cannot rely on such carve-outs. Thus, developers in the EU are prohibited from collecting personal data via scraping or using personal data for AI training purposes unless the data subject consents or they can find another lawful basis. Consequently, developers do not consider countries where the GDPR applies a business-friendly jurisdiction for data acquisition or AI development activities.

1.8.4   Processing

Under the GDPR, "processing" means any operation on personal data including collection, recording, organization, structuring, storage, adaptation or alteration, retrieval, consultation, use, disclosure by transmission, dissemination or otherwise making available, alignment or combination, restriction, erasure, or destruction. If an AI developer aggregates or de-identifies personal data that is subject to the GDPR, the developer engages in "processing" and must find a lawful basis to justify the activity.

1.8.5   Restrictions on personal data processing

By default, processing of personal data is prohibited under Articles 6(1) and 9(1) of the GDPR, "verboten" in German. Therefore, AI developers have to obtain informed, voluntary, express, and specific consent before they process any data that pertains to an identifiable person, even if they do not know the person's name or contact information, unless they can claim another lawful basis. Developers can also process personal data based on legitimate interests, but they have to assess whether such interests are overridden by the interests or fundamental rights and freedoms of the data subject, and accordingly offer opt-out rights.

1.8.6   Data minimization, purpose limitation, fairness

Once companies have satisfied themselves that they can justify data processing under the GDPR, they still have to comply with data minimization, transparency, fairness, and deletion protocols. Developers must not use data that was originally collected for a different purpose, unless they determine and document that the new use is compatible with the original use and the data subjects have been sufficiently notified. Companies find similar purpose limitation requirements in other laws, including the California Consumer Privacy Act (CCPA), according to which businesses must ensure that their collection, use, retention, and sharing of a consumer's personal information is reasonably necessary and proportionate to achieve the purposes for which the personal information was collected or processed, or for another disclosed purpose that is compatible with the context in which the personal information was collected. Therefore, AI developers have to examine the circumstances under which personal data was originally collected before they can decide whether they may include it in AI data training sets. Going forward, companies have to consider proactively notifying data subjects about such plans and potentially seek consent where required by law.

1.8.7   Data subject rights

Under the GDPR, individual data subjects have rights to access, correct, and erase data about them as well as a right not to be subject to individual decisions based solely on automated processing, including profiling, which produce legal effects or affect them in similarly significant ways. Developers are concerned that these rights extend to training data as well as AI input and output, which could hamper AI operation, even if AI itself does not typically contain any personal data. If a data subject complains that AI output contains factually incorrect personal data, for example, the developers or providers may not be able to arrange for corrections, given that they cannot predict, explain, or control how the AI arrived at that particular result. Developers could technically try to correct all information about a particular data subject in the training data set and then retrain the AI with the improved data set, but even such enormous efforts cannot eliminate all inaccuracies in output of Large Language Models

(LLMs) that deploy probabilistic methods, because their output is by definition always only probably correct and probably occasionally incorrect.

1.8.8   Data protection impact assessments

Under Articles 35 and 36 of the GDPR, companies have to conduct data protection impact assessments (DPIAs) concerning the development and use of AI. In the context of DPIAs, companies must consider all rights and freedoms of data subjects, not only privacy interests. Historically, Europeans enacted data protection laws to address all threats to human rights and interests emanating from computers, which is why data protection laws are by design also relevant for all other concerns relating to AI, beyond data privacy.

The German State of Hessen enacted the world's first data protection law in 1970 due to growing concerns regarding dangers of automated data processing for individual freedoms. Hessians feared that George Orwell's forecast for 1984 could become reality when the police started to use computers to build profiles on citizens and their social connections to detect domestic terrorism conspiracies. They objected to being observed like "glass citizens" and controlled by an omniscient "big brother" – a computerized government. Therefore, they decided to regulate automated data processing like other dangerous activities and generally prohibited personal data processing, except with a lawful basis. Other jurisdictions enacted similar laws, and the European Community eventually harmonized member state laws in Directive 95/46/EC, the predecessor to the GDPR (which took effect on May 25, 2018).

1.8.9   Territorial applicability of the GDPR

Companies have to comply with the GDPR if they are established in the one of the member states of the European Union (EU), the European Economic Area (EEA – which also includes Iceland, Liechtenstein, and Norway), or the UK (together "EEA+"). If a company opens a branch office or operates servers in an EEA+ member state, it will be considered established there. Data protection authorities in the EEA+ take the position that even one employee acting in a country could constitute an establishment of a company incorporated elsewhere if that employee is involved in the data processing activity at issue. Companies that are established outside the EEA+ have to comply with the GDPR if they monitor persons in the EEA+ or collect personal data from individuals in the EEA+ in the context of providing goods or services, but not if they avoid such activities in the EEA+. Therefore, multinationals should consider conducting data acquisition, machine learning, and other AI development activities outside the EEA+. Some multinationals have already announced that they will not offer access to their AI to individual users in the EEA+ given that this could trigger the applicability of the GDPR.

1.8.10   GDPR compliance action items

Companies that have to comply with the GDPR should address the following top ten priority compliance requirements concerning AI:

(a) Issue privacy notices with detailed disclosures addressing requirements prescribed in Articles 12 and 13 of the GDPR to AI users. According to Article 14 of the GDPR, companies are also required to inform data subjects from whom they collect data indirectly, for example, via scraping data from publicly available websites. They may be able to reach some of those data subjects with disclosures in public website privacy statements, but realistically, they cannot directly send privacy notices to all data subjects about whom they may receive personal data via scraping public websites, because they do not have sufficient contact information.

(b) Document data protection impact assessments (DPIAs) and privacy-by-design measures concerning AI, including data minimization measures, removal or redaction of personal data in training data sets, filters on input and output, and contractual use restrictions.

(c) Prevent children from providing personal data without parental consent, where such consent is required, and protect children from exposure to harmful content generated by AI.

(d) Sign data processing agreements with AI providers and other processors. Consider using the Standard Contractual Clauses that the EU Commission promulgated in 2021 for international data transfers and additional or alternative compliance vehicles such as Binding Corporate Rules and registering for the EU–U.S. Data Privacy Framework. Document data transfer impact assessments concerning data protection levels in jurisdictions outside the EEA+.

(e) Designate a data protection officer (DPO) and notify all competent authorities, unless the company can avoid processing significant amounts of sensitive personal data. German companies must designate a DPO if they have 20 or more employees. Other EEA+ member states impose different thresholds. Companies that are established in a particular EEA+ member state have to notify only one locally competent authority of the DPO designation, whereas a U.S. company is required to notify all 40+ authorities in the EEA+ of the locations from which it receives personal data if the company is subject to the GDPR.

(f) Upgrade and document data security measures as well as data retention and deletion periods in records of processing activities pertaining to training data, AI input, output, and databases.

(g) Establish processes to manage data subject requests for information on data processing activities, copies of personal data, correction, restrictions, and erasure, and comply with objections to automated decision-making and data processing based on legitimate interests.

(h) Appoint a local representative in the EU for entities outside the EEA+; pay the required annual registration fee for data controllers in the UK or designate a local representative for an entity outside the UK.

(i) Address risks of inclusion of inaccurate information in output that users could consider personal data, including with update and correction measures and contractual means to require users to verify AI output before relying on it as personal data or factual information.

(j) Document compliance with each applicable GDPR requirement in a dossier to demonstrate how the company complies, as required by Article 5(2) of the GDPR.

1.9   Data residency and retention

Besides privacy and data protection laws, AI developers and users also have to comply with data residency and data retention requirements. Russia enacted the world's first broad data residency law effective September 1, 2015, in the form of an amendment to its general data protection law. Kazakhstan, the People's Republic of China, and Indonesia followed suit and also added data residency requirements to their data protection laws.

Privacy, data protection, data retention, and data residency (also known as "data localization" or "data sovereignty") are concepts that are often confused. But, privacy and data protection laws on the one hand, and data residency and retention requirements on the other hand, actually have completely different purposes and effects. With data residency and retention requirements, governments try to ensure that government officials, courts, auditors, and others are able to gain access to data when they need it. Privacy and data protection laws, on the other hand, are intended to restrict availability and access to personal data in the interest of protecting individual data subject rights. Data transfer restrictions, for example, limit companies' ability to transfer personal data from one jurisdiction to another. European countries have been restricting international data transfers for decades in the interest of privacy protection. But, true data privacy laws do not include any requirements to keep data for a minimum period of time (data retention) or in a particular location (data residency), because such requirements are detrimental to privacy interests. Data privacy laws are about protecting personal data from access and use by governments and companies. Data retention and data residency laws secure access to personal data. They are anti-privacy laws.

Companies are caught in the crossfire of data protection, data retention, and data residency laws, which impose contrary and often conflicting requirements. European-style data protection laws require companies to delete data that they no longer legitimately need, so companies have to observe maximum data retention periods. Other laws can specify minimum data retention periods, during which companies must retain data and make it available on request, for example to tax authorities and law enforcement officials. Also, under accounting standards and contracts, and due to operational necessities, companies must keep data for a certain minimum data retention period, such as to keep account information available for users, retain proof to support or defend against potential claims, and track employee performance for career management purposes. Thus, for every category of data, companies have to consider three types of data retention periods – a minimum required by law, a period desired by the company for business reasons, and a maximum permitted by law. To make things even more complicated, these requirements vary by jurisdiction and do not only apply on a per-record basis, but per category of data and purpose of processing. If a particular document serves more than one purpose or jurisdiction, it may be required to be partially retained and partially deleted. On top of this, under U.S. law, companies have to preserve evidence that could be relevant for litigation under certain circumstances (litigation hold), which will override regular data retention policies.

Many companies have capitulated before the overwhelming complexity of creating a legally compliant record retention program and simply store data indefinitely. Data hoarders cater to a "what if we need it" mindset and, given the magnitude of risk arising under laws that require minimum retention periods, these companies have decided that violating the maximum retention period requirements under data protection laws is the lesser evil. This has resulted in a continual increase of stored data and made companies more vulnerable to data security breaches in addition to raising costs of document production in litigation. On the other hand, companies that have taken this approach may now have a host of training data at their disposal for AI development, to which companies that complied with deletion requirements do not have access.

In light of the prohibitive costs associated with "getting it right" and the unacceptable risks resulting from making no effort at all, some companies try to strike a balance by preparing retention schedules and protocols for key records. Instead of determining the exact minimum and maximum requirements, companies can pick a number of years that should satisfy most minimum requirements (*e.g.*, seven or ten years) and yet is not too close to "indefinite," and then apply shorter retention periods to record types whose retention is particularly costly or risky, for example, email, credit card numbers, system logs, and certain paper records. Alternatively, companies can start applying deletion requirements on a department-by-department basis and tackle "low-hanging fruit" first – for example HR and accounting departments, which often have systems in place and industry standards to guide them. Given the avalanche of lawsuits that plaintiffs' firms have filed in the United States to challenge companies' use of training data, AI developers, providers, and users should review their existing data retention and deletion policies and consider deleting databases with questionable origins or whether the company cannot justify retention in light of deletion requirements under privacy or data protection laws.

1.10   Contracts and industry standards

While governments are pondering legislation and regulations, businesses will agree on legal frameworks for the development, provisioning, and use of AI by way of contracts and industry standards. Practitioners have to consider opportunities to shape the legal situation pertaining to their use of AI by way of contracts with AI developers, providers, and users. Also, companies have to react to demands for contract terms they receive from business partners and consider how existing contracts affect their ability to use AI. For example, companies that have amassed libraries of books, code, and other content have to consider whether they can use such content for purposes of AI training under existing agreements. Recruiters, business consultants, and payroll providers have to analyze whether they are free to deploy AI to perform services for their customers under existing contracts.

2 Starting an AI law compliance program

When you set out to design and implement a compliance program focused on particular laws, business processes, or risks, you face a number of threshold decisions and preparatory tasks, including the following:

- Deciding which person or team to put in charge of compliance.
- Preparing a task list while identifying relevant facts, laws, and requirements.
- Defining priorities based on business objectives, enforcement risk exposure, and ease of compliance.
- Gathering buy-in from senior leaders.
- Working with internal stakeholders and outside advisors.
- Executing the task list.

2.1 Take charge

Someone needs to be in charge. If your business is a one-person sole proprietorship, then you are in charge. In larger organizations, there are typically a number of individual candidates or departments that could take charge of compliance with respect to Artificial Intelligence (AI), including lawyers, information technology (IT) staff, data protection officers, and general compliance program managers. Also, product researchers and developers are required to ensure compliance with respect to their activities. AI users in the HR, production, sales, and marketing departments could be tasked with ensuring compliance pertaining to particular systems and use cases. Each of these groups tends to have different approaches, strengths, and limitations. Here are some factors to consider as you look for the right person or team:

2.1.1   DPOs and privacy professionals

Data protection officers and privacy professionals are focused on ensuring compliance with data protection and privacy laws. Under data protection laws in Europe, companies have to designate individuals as data protection officers (DPOs) who can monitor compliance without conflicts of interest and who are capable of understanding data processing systems and applicable data protection laws. Many DPOs and privacy professionals are not trained attorneys, however, and tend to be less familiar with other laws implicated by AI, such as intellectual property, tort, computer interference, and anti-discrimination laws.

2.1.2   Lawyers

In-house attorneys in corporate legal departments usually take an advisory role and inform others in the organization what applicable laws require. Depending on company culture and individual styles, the legal department may advise proactively or upon request. Lawyers are trained to interpret and apply laws, but not all lawyers are technology-savvy or good managers of compliance programs.

2.1.3   IT professionals

Members of the information technology (IT) department are technology-savvy, but they may not find it easy to understand and apply laws. IT professionals are trained in deploying and maintaining equipment, software, and services that other groups use, including HR, production, sales, and marketing. The IT department supports these other groups and provides technology that aids other departments' business objectives. The IT department usually establishes and implements protocols to protect systems and data from unauthorized access (by deploying data security measures), but does not typically decide access privileges for individuals or address legal compliance matters.

2.1.4   Product developers

Computer and data scientists who develop AI are uniquely positioned to mitigate risks of violating laws, because they understand AI better and earlier than providers and users. They control the selection of code and training data. They can identify and ensure compliance with open source software licenses and terms governing access to data on public websites, which is restricted by copyright, privacy rights, and computer interference laws. If they select appropriately diverse training data, developers can significantly reduce the risk that AI output later contributes to violations of anti-discrimination laws. During the initial design and training process, developers can apply guardrails and risk mitigation measures. Developers have the power to set AI on a path that will ultimately comply or conflict with laws. But, computer and data scientists are driven by the objective to optimize functionalities and capabilities of AI. They may perceive compliance requirements as an obstacle that conflicts with their primary goals.

2.1.5   Auditors and compliance officers

Some companies have internal audit or compliance professionals, who are concerned with monitoring and enforcing compliance with laws and internal policies. Auditors are focused on verifying that rules of existing compliance programs are adhered to. But, they do not typically define the rules, and may not have the right expertise to do so. Also, you lose an extra pair of eyes if you have the same person create and audit a compliance program.

2.1.6   AI users

Another option is to select individuals from data user groups within a company, such as HR or marketing. But, like developers, users of AI tend to perceive compliance requirements as an obstacle that conflicts with their primary goals of completing tasks and achieving business objectives with AI.

2.1.7   New committee or officer(s)

In many businesses, the person in charge of compliance pertaining to AI will likely come from one of the above departments or areas of specialization. Larger companies with significant exposure or interest relating to AI may also decide to create a new compliance program or department.

2.2   Govern

Companies should consider forming committees and working groups consisting of stakeholders and subject matter experts with diverse backgrounds and interests to increase chances of identifying compliance risks relating to AI. This step seems particularly compelling as an initial measure, while everyone is still grappling with how to position the organization with respect to AI. Leaders who are wary of creating new layers of bureaucracy could emphasize the temporary nature of the committee assignments. They could evaluate from time to time whether a committee approach is effective or if individual officers should take over.

Particularly for AI development, but also for AI acquisition initiatives, companies should consider creating multi-stakeholder review committees and designating an individual employee as a steward for each system. The committee should ideally reflect diverse backgrounds and opinions to effectively identify and eliminate unconscious biases and define protocols and processes. Data acquisition is a particularly complex and risky area that should be guided by a separate process approved by committee. For each system and data acquisition project, an individual employee should take responsibility as steward and monitor compliance, the effectiveness of guardrails, the volume of complaints, and any new concerns regarding output. The individual data steward should also sign off on the categorization of a particular system as AI or deterministically programmed, as a basis for legal review and advice on compliance parameters. Separately, a team of researchers (often referred to as the "red team") should continuously test AI systems for quality deficits, safety risks, and security vulnerabilities.

Many organizations prioritize inclusion and diversity when they appoint employees in AI governance roles. Members of disadvantaged minority groups tend to be particularly good at detecting unconscious and illegal biases or measures that indirectly discriminate and affect them personally, or other groups. Attorneys, IT professionals, data scientists, and AI users bring different subject matter expertise to the table. Employees from different regions and cultures are sensitive to additional concerns that could otherwise be overlooked. When employers select candidates for governance committee positions, however, they must not discriminate against individual candidates based on race, gender, age, or other protected criteria, as with all other employment decisions.

Smaller companies may have to rely more on external sources of diversity guidance and internally put an employee in charge on a part-time basis. If a company has a legal department, attorneys are usually involved. Often, the legal counsel takes the lead regarding compliance with laws. But, the ideal candidate does not necessarily have to be a lawyer.

2.3   Assign accountability

In order to drive accountability, companies should consider designating an individual as a steward for each system. The individual system steward could initially determine whether a particular system qualifies as AI under applicable definitions and then conduct and document an assessment of compliance risks. The system steward should also be tasked with monitoring performance and output of AI on an ongoing basis and flag concerns to in-house legal counsels, data protection officers, or general compliance officers.

For internally developed AI, the project manager or an individual developer might be a good system steward. For any systems, key users should also be considered for a steward role.

Individual system stewards should ensure that humans are accountable for AI. Stewards should remain closely focused on each system and ready to step in and address compliance concerns or report risks to the person or department who is in charge of compliance with respect to AI for the entire organization. The compliance manager for the entire organization could rely to some extent on systems stewards for ongoing systems monitoring and ensure that systems stewards are replaced if they leave the company, become overwhelmed with too many assignments, or underperform in their role.

2.4   Work effectively with internal stakeholders and outside advisors

To obtain sufficient resources and support from stakeholders within a company, you have to answer the "Why" question: Why is a compliance program important? Developers, providers, and users of AI can be liable for harm and violations of law that AI causes. Thus, all companies understand compliance as an important matter of risk management and avoiding sanctions and liability.

Additionally, for AI developers and providers, compliance can be a sales topic. They can point to AI guardrails and features that support compliance purposes as a competitive differentiator when they promote their AI offerings. For example, employers in New York City are required to evaluate automated employment decision tools ("AEDT") to assess the likelihood of disparate impact and discrimination based on gender, race, or ethnicity. They have to engage independent auditors and will be more likely to buy a tool from a provider that can produce sample audit reports to demonstrate that the employer will likely pass any audit of its practices. Also, for AI providers, data security law compliance is a key precondition to selling products and services. When you start implementing a compliance program in a company, it can be very helpful to prepare a brief white paper in FAQ format to raise awareness and gain support among key stakeholders within the organization. This can be a differentiator for sales purposes.

Most companies also turn to outside advisors. For example, they need external counsel for advice on legal requirements beyond their home jurisdiction. Except at very large multinational enterprises, in-house counsel find it too difficult and time consuming to determine the exact nature and details of formal and substantive compliance obligations in other countries, where laws may be presented in unfamiliar formats and languages. Also, management may need to turn to external subject matter experts for specialist questions beyond core expertise within their organization.

In this context, they experience one particular challenge when working with outside advisors on compliance matters: every subject matter expert (data security consultant, technology vendor, or local lawyer in a particular jurisdiction) is familiar with facts, risks, and rules in the expert's area of specialty and takes these particularly seriously. Companies tend to have a limited budget and cannot hire an array of experts or address all requirements at once and with the same rigor and effort. Companies need to prioritize.

If you hire coordinated global teams, they may be able to assist with prioritizing among the disciplines they are engaged to cover, but even their abilities are limited and they cannot be expected to take all fundamental considerations into account that can make or break a company, *e.g.*, how to secure operational continuity, revenue, and funding.

If you hire individual advisors rather than a coordinated team, such individuals are usually not of much help with respect to prioritizing. Each expert will tend to consider issues in her jurisdiction or area of expertise the most pressing of all, which creates a significant chance that the importance of a particular risk or local law requirement ends up over- or understated. Therefore, it can be helpful to ask outside advisors not only about substantive and formal requirements, but also about practical issues, such as whether particular requirements are observed in practice or only honored in the breach, whether challenges by regulatory or private plaintiffs are common, and what risks and problems other companies have run into in connection with the particular requirement at issue. Answers to such questions help put things into perspective and help companies prioritize tasks.

2.5   Mind tools and automation

A number of "legal tech" businesses offer software tools and other technical solutions to help companies address compliance requirements, such as upload filters to reduce copyright infringement, image blurring software to mitigate privacy impacts, and online forms to document data protection impact assessments (DPIAs). Companies with mature compliance programs can benefit from automating recurring tasks. But, every company must first assess its particular compliance needs, options, and preferences before resorting to technical solutions. For example, a company that receives only a handful of data access requests every year, from different jurisdictions and from different groups of data subjects (*e.g.*, employees and customers), may be better off manually processing such requests, given that initial discretion may be necessary in each case and the configuration of a tool (which could handle requests automatically) takes up resources, too.

It is worth noting that companies that have prematurely deployed tools to conduct DPIAs have become suffocated by too many records that are neither legally required nor practically helpful, and the superfluous records and activities sometime conceal situations where a deeper assessment was required. While data security measures have a single goal (prevent unauthorized access to data) and they are therefore relatively easy to automate, other laws are more nuanced, requiring individual balancing decisions, and thus present much greater challenges to automation. For example, data protection laws require balancing of legitimate business interests with potentially overriding data subject rights. Under copyright laws, developers may copy and adapt works without a license if they satisfy a complex, multi-factor fair use test. Moreover, AI law is a relatively new field for most organizations. Consequently, they have much less experience and historic data to rely on for decision-making and they may have to change course quickly and often as they confront new AI use cases, risks, and laws.

Even where a technical measure offers an undoubtedly effective solution, companies should determine first whether the measure is required or desirable from a business perspective. For example, face-blurring software may be effective at protecting privacy. But, some organizations may justify the deployment of AI-assisted security cameras with facial recognition systems to keep persons off the premises who have previously made threats or attacked employees or patrons. Also, a developer of self-driving cars must balance safety and privacy interests before opting for face-blurring measures that could render AI less effective at identifying pedestrians and hamper evasive maneuvers for safety purposes. Moreover, users of tools for gap and impact assessments can be disappointed when they realize how much effort the initial configuration of the tool takes up, that they have to gather and enter a lot of relevant information, and that they still have to make the ultimate decisions whether risks are acceptable. Therefore, companies should carefully determine at the outset what specific problem they can solve with a particular tool, whether the solution provided by the tool is legally required and the best option for the company, and how the costs and benefits associated with the tool compare to costs and benefits of manual or other approaches.

!	Action Items

- Task individuals with responsibility for particular AI systems and a person or department to oversee compliance for the entire organization.
- Convene a diverse group of stakeholders and subject matter experts to help identify opportunities and risks.
- Design and test the compliance program before you automate or rely on tools too much.

2.6   Prepare a task list

Once someone is in charge and you made basic decisions on who is working on AI compliance, it is time to prepare a list of tasks and keep track of implementation status. Creating and monitoring such lists help prioritization, planning (budgets, achievements), management of complex situations (*e.g.*, involving several jurisdictions and different types of AI), and transitioning projects from one employee to another. On a task list, you can keep tabs on formal compliance requirements (*e.g.*, impact assessment documentation, audit reports, notices regarding automated decision-making, vendor contracts, designation of systems stewards) and substantive tasks (*e.g.*, developing and testing guardrails for AI products, assigning and limiting access privileges, deploying encryption technologies).

For example, a multinational group with companies in the EU, Japan, PRC, and U.S. may have the following items on its initial task list – perhaps supplemented by columns for status, action items, and responsible persons:

Table 2.1   *Sample compliance task list*

	Compliance Task	Purpose
i.	Form an AI governance committee	Manage opportunities and risks
ii.	Issue protocols and approval processes for data and AI acquisition and use of AI	Mitigate risks
iii.	Take inventory of AI, databases, and data flows	Compile facts for impact assessments, notices, agreements; satisfy record-keeping requirements
iv.	Designate an individual employee as systems steward for each AI	Assure human accountability, mitigate risks
v.	Conduct and document impact assessments	Compliance with law, risk mitigation
vi.	Update intra-group commercial agreements (to justify transfer pricing for AI usage for tax purposes) and data transfer agreements based on EU Standard Contractual Clauses and other measures to legitimize international data transfers, within the group and with vendors and customers	Compliance with law, overcome legal restrictions on international data transfers
vii.	Create, update, and translate notices directed at consumers and individual representatives of corporate customers and business partners concerning automated decision-making and data processing; determine how best to obtain and document consent and honor objections and opt-out choices	Satisfy notice, choice, and consent requirements
viii.	Review or prepare notices directed at employees and candidates with respect to automated decision-making and processing of personal data, including:	Satisfy notice requirements

Compliance Task	Purpose
• Job application processing	
• Monitoring tools and investigations	
• Evaluations, compensation, and promotion	

2.7   Take stock of AI and laws

To define tasks for your company, you have to determine what AI you use, what laws apply, what the laws require, and how your company can best satisfy the requirements (where the law gives you options or where resource limitations force prioritization). You could prepare a task list for your company as you read through the remainder of this Field Guide, where you can find examples of typical requirements and tasks.

Finding and analyzing all AI that an organization uses, internally and externally, can feel like a Sisyphean task if you work for a large organization or any business with an international scope. Employees use search engines, maps, and myriad other publicly available online services that are likely based on AI to some extent. Also, many corporate services and internal systems may use some AI functionality. Moreover, by the time you have taken an inventory of existing AI deployments, training databases, development projects, and use cases, the organization has probably swapped out a few systems, acquired and spun off companies, entered new jurisdictions, and found new opportunities to deploy AI, while several new laws and regulations specifically concerning AI or data processing may have been enacted.

Don't let "perfect" become the enemy of "good." At the outset, consider where you already know that your business develops and uses AI. At a minimum, you should prepare a brief summary with basic information on your key use cases, geographical location of servers, and who has access (*e.g.*, employees, departments, and third party vendors). If you have international operations, you will also need to know names, addresses, and headcount of all your legal entities and branches.

If you are working for a small or medium-sized company, it should not take you more than a few hours to prepare such an initial summary. You can go to the IT, procurement, and accounting departments to obtain basic information on systems purchased and deployed. The legal department should have a list of subsidiaries. HR should know headcount. That is enough to get started.

If your company is subject to the GDPR, you may find – or have to create – more formal and detailed records of data processing activities, including:

- names and contact details of your company or companies, their representatives in the EU and UK, and their data protection officer, if any;
- purposes of the data processing;
- categories of data and data subjects;
- categories of recipients to whom you disclose data, including processors (and customers, if your company acts as a processor) and recipients in third countries or international organizations;
- international transfers and documentation of suitable safeguards in place, including the identification of that third country or international organization;
- time limits for retention and erasure;
- general descriptions of technical and organizational security measures (TOMs).

Also, your company may have conducted data protection impact assessments for purposes of GDPR compliance, which can provide valuable information for your AI inventory.

Larger companies sometimes conduct more elaborate assessments and audits, often with the help – and sometimes at the initiative – of outside advisors. In complex multinational organizations, this can be beneficial and even necessary to get a solid grip on facts concerning AI use cases and compliance. However, such exercises can also take a long time, use a lot of resources, and produce reports with overwhelming detail that do not directly translate into improving the organization's compliance status. Consider starting with a high-level inventory unless you are fairly sure that your company is past the initial compliance phase and you can stomach a full-blown systems mapping exercise.

2.8   Prioritize

Given the rapid pace at which AI technologies and regulations develop, it is usually most effective to design and implement a compliance program in phases. Companies that start out by trying to take a complete inventory of all AI deployments and applicable legal requirements often find the challenge overwhelming and become paralyzed. Focus first on high risks and easily addressable requirements in both the design and implementation phase. That way, you can score a "quick win" and build rapport with other teams during the initial stages of the program. Start with implementing high-priority tasks while you are still refining the design of the program and building out your task list. Compile a list of known compliance requirements that your organization and your peers and competitors already try to satisfy, or that are actively enforced.

When you identify compliance gaps in high-risk areas, take action immediately. For example, if you find that data scientists inappropriately scraped data from public websites in violation of computer interference laws (such as the U.S. Computer Fraud and Abuse Act), data protection regulations, or copyright laws, or if you find databases with questionable origins, you may determine with your legal counsel that it may be appropriate to erase such data immediately, before a lawsuit or government investigation requires you to preserve and produce records under litigation holds.

After you have addressed the most urgent risks, then continue building your task list and addressing the tasks one by one. In parallel, you should think strategically about what is needed to achieve more difficult goals. As you build and address your task list, you should document your objectives and priorities with respect to AI and compliance. Some companies view compliance pertaining to AI like any other legal requirement: they want to do only what is legally required – the bare minimum that is commonly done in their industry and market segment. Other companies – particularly companies that develop and provide AI – view compliance features as a potential competitive differentiator; consequently, they want to do whatever their customers expect or desire, and perhaps more than the competition.

Also, with respect to particular aspects of compliance, the objectives vary. For example, some companies depend heavily on AI functionality, for example, for purposes of direct marketing. Such companies may want to collect and use personal data to the maximum extent permitted in each jurisdiction, whatever the costs. Other companies may be content to find and comply with the strictest requirement worldwide and implement a uniform compliance protocol in the interest of uniformity and cost savings. It is important to document and communicate these objectives efficiently to employees.

Based on an initial assessment of applicable requirements and your objectives, you can select an approach that suits your organization and situation:

- Proactive or reactive? It is usually less risky, easier, and cheaper to take proactive steps to avoid a problem than to cope with a lawsuit, investigation, or negative press campaign. At the same time, only a fraction of potential problems materialize. If cost containment is a key driver and your organization views compliance with laws pertaining to AI as just another legal obligation, you may consider a risk–benefit analysis and the 80–20 rule (Pareto Principle). A relatively smaller percentage of potential problems (perhaps 20 percent in some cases) is responsible for the vast majority of adverse impacts (perhaps 80 percent in some cases – but this is just an estimate). Conversely, companies can cover perhaps 80 percent of their problems with 20 percent of the budget it would take to address all problems. To address the remaining 20 percent of problems, which may not even be the most serious problems, the company would have to expend 80 percent of the total potential budget. Based on these considerations, companies first try to find and rectify those problems that are most likely to result in major issues as well the problems that require the least amount of effort and resources to fix.
- Some problems (*e.g.*, outdated privacy notices that do not address rights to object to automated decision-making) are easier and cheaper to fix than other problems (*e.g.*, a lack of budget for encryption technology or the need to add meaningful human decision-making to resumé screening processes). Companies on a budget may find it easier to start with "low-hanging fruit." To some extent, you can assess what your main competitors are doing by reviewing their website privacy notices. AI users can ask providers and developers for recommendations and guidance on their websites. Then, you can determine whether your company is legally required to adopt particu-

lar compliance measures observed or recommended and then follow suit. This approach by no means guarantees full compliance, but it can help a company catch up to industry standards relatively quickly and with modest resources.

- If your company is or wants to become an industry leader, you have to consider a more comprehensive assessment of legal requirements and business needs. You can poll stakeholders in various departments (including legal, data protection office, HR, IT, sales, product management, and procurement) to prepare a list of company-specific priorities concerning AI. You can also subscribe to legal and trade publications, attend conferences, follow guidance from government authorities, possibly even proactively seek guidance from authorities, and monitor enforcement and litigation cases to obtain a broader picture of the compliance and risk landscape concerning AI. You may also consider proactively briefing law and policy makers, proposing new legislation, or submitting comments, either directly or via industry associations, to authorities seeking input during rule-making proceedings.

- In terms of following guidance from government authorities, it is important to determine to what extent your business is exposed to action from governments. A regulated entity (*e.g.*, a bank or telecommunications service provider) usually has to take its regulator's views seriously whether based on laws or not because it depends on the goodwill of its regulator in many respects. Entities that are neither regulated nor sell primarily to regulated entities, however, are freer to take their own positions and views. Employees at such entities will typically ask not only what the views of a particular government entity are, but also if and how such views are enforced. This is particularly important with respect to gauging the relevance of official guidance from government authorities abroad. European authorities, for example, have taken relatively extreme positions on various topics over many years without any enforcement activities that could have resulted in "reality checks" in court. A company that readily follows the official guidance at the expense of missing out on business opportunities may regret doing so if the guidance is not followed in practice or is even at some point challenged and invalidated in courts of law.

- Keep in mind that a company may find different approaches appropriate for a particular jurisdiction or part of its business. For example, a company with a large employee population and hostile union leadership or works council in a subsidiary would seem well advised to be particularly proactive with respect to AI deployment that can affect workers' rights. A start-up company with a particularly sensitive AI product (*e.g.*, a facial recognition product that excludes patrons from public places on security grounds) may go out of its way to achieve or surpass compliance requirements with respect to its products, but it may decide that following industry standards suffices with respect to the rights of its few employees. Workers' rights concerning AI may be even less of a concern for a company that is still managed and operated largely by a group of founders who have a significant financial stake in the company and hence a relatively strong interest in minimizing compliance costs and efforts.

2.9   Identify key legal requirements

As noted in the first chapter of this Field Guide, only relatively few jurisdictions have enacted AI-specific laws as of 2023. Yet, companies have to comply with myriad laws around the world that address AI in one way or another. Even very large and compliance-oriented companies struggle to keep up to date. Smaller organizations have to establish priorities and a system to ensure that they are capable of complying with key requirements – even if they may not be able to identify each and every law, or provisions in relevant laws, in detail.

2.9.1   Which laws are particularly relevant for AI and your company?

AI developers, providers, and users have to comply with a variety of laws that may have different histories and public policy motivations. For example, companies have to comply with computer interference laws (including the U.S. Computer Fraud and Abuse Act), copyright laws, data protection regulations, and privacy laws when acquiring data for AI training. Users of AI have to comply with confidentiality obligations and data protection laws concerning input they provide to AI and also consider whether their prompts and directions to AI increase the risk that output can infringe copyrights, privacy, and other rights and interests of others. Additionally, developers, providers, and users of AI have to consider AI-specific risks that could result in harm to humans or property, triggering liability under criminal and tort laws. In Chapter 1 of this Field Guide, you were provided an overview regarding AI law, and in Chapter

4 you will find an A-Z of risks to consider for purposes of conducting and documenting AI impact assessments. Once you have identified particularly relevant risks relating to a particular system or AI use case, you can more easily prepare a list of laws with which your company is required to comply, in order to avoid or mitigate such risks.

2.9.2   Which laws apply to your company based on subject matter limitations?

Some laws apply directly only to certain types of entities. For example, European data protection laws do not typically apply to data processing by national security agencies or by private individuals in the course of a purely personal or household activity (*e.g.*, what someone asks a chatbot or shares about friends within their immediate family after opting out of allowing the use of prompts for training purposes). Healthcare-related data privacy laws in the United States (*e.g.*, HIPAA) apply only to certain "covered entities" and their "business associates," such as medical doctors, health insurers, and certain service providers. Some laws relating to financial or telecommunications services apply only to banks or telecommunications providers, respectively. Anti-spam laws tend to focus on for-profit, commercial enterprises and contain exceptions for political and non-profit organizations.

Even if a certain law does not apply to your business, it may nevertheless be relevant if it applies to your business partners or customers. Most businesses, though, are able to remove a significant number of laws from consideration based on the type of business sectors, organizations, or situations such laws cover.

2.9.3   Which laws apply to your company based on territorial limitations?

The United Nations recognizes more than 190 countries in the world. Within each country, you may be dealing with several different jurisdictions, including 50 states within the United States. Companies usually take a hard look at which jurisdictions' requirements they have to prioritize.

Under customary international law, every sovereign country is free to legislate on whatever it is interested in. There is no "world constitution" or treaty that limits what countries can cover in their national laws.

But, historically, many countries have traditionally limited their laws to apply to persons on their territory and companies that are incorporated or registered in their country or that maintain a physical presence with employees, offices, servers, or other equipment there.

Under international treaties, certain types of copyright laws and other intellectual property laws are territorial and apply only to infringements that occur on the legislating country's territory, *e.g.*, where the infringer makes an infringing copy. Also, computer interference laws such as the U.S. Computer Fraud and Abuse Act tend to protect only computers physically located on the legislating country's territory; if someone hacks into computers abroad to scrape data for AI training purposes, the hacker typically violates only the computer interference laws of the country where the scraped computers reside and not the laws of the country where the hacker acts.

Increasingly, countries apply consumer and privacy protection laws to persons and entities abroad to protect local consumers from harm. For example, data privacy laws may apply to any company that collects data remotely via targeted websites (as indicated by country-specific URLs, languages, localized content, or local phone numbers) or even just on the basis that the foreign company collects data on residents of the legislating country. Internet service providers, multinational enterprises, and many other companies with more or less direct business connections to other countries find that many countries' privacy laws apply to some of their data processing activities. But, many companies with a domestic focus can rule out most countries' laws because they are not permitted to or able to do business in other jurisdictions due to regulatory restrictions (*e.g.*, local banks or hospitals) or resource limitations (*e.g.*, local construction companies).

Under European Union law, member states generally may not apply their national laws extraterritorially to companies in other member states. This is intended to make it easier for companies based in the EEA to do business across national borders everywhere in the Common Market. An EEA-based AI provider has to comply primarily with the national laws of the EEA member state where it operates its system or maintains a significant, physical presence, even if it offers its service online to other EEA member states (over the Internet or otherwise).

This privilege is not available, however, to companies outside the EEA. A U.S.-based AI provider with customers throughout the EEA has to comply with the national laws of every EEA member state where its customers reside. If the U.S. provider incorporates a subsidiary, however, to become the sole contracting party and data controller for all European customers, then the new subsidiary would have to comply only with the data protection laws of the one jurisdiction where it is incorporated. Also, it could claim privileges under the "country of origin principle" with respect to other types of laws of other EEA member states where it does not maintain establishments. Moreover, EEA-based entities typically are subject only to supervision and enforcement by authorities in the member state where they are established, whereas a U.S. company may have to notify more than 45 different national authorities in national languages if it appoints a data protection officer or suffers a data security breach. Companies operating in the United States may be able to invoke protections under the U.S. Constitution's "Commerce Clause" against state laws that discriminate against, or unduly burden, interstate commerce. Such jurisdictional privileges provide some companies with a planning opportunity to actively influence which laws apply to them or which authorities are likely to assert jurisdiction over them. For all of these reasons, it is important for companies to carefully select their territorial footprint and corporate structure.

2.9.4   Which laws can be enforced against your company?

Most practitioners find it difficult to answer this additional threshold question with reasonable certainty, but it is helpful to try to answer it, in order to prioritize international compliance efforts. As a general matter, countries cannot easily enforce their laws against your company if you do not have a physical presence, assets, or employees in their territory. Under sovereignty principles established by customary international law, national governments must not send officials across borders to issue warnings, collect fines, or make arrests. They are also not supposed to send orders or official letters with warnings or threats across borders without seeking consent from the home jurisdiction of the enforcement target, because this would amount to exercising regulatory powers in another country. Some countries (*e.g.*, EEA member states) cooperate relatively closely on some topics, but more often than not it is difficult and burdensome to take enforcement actions against companies in other countries.

Private plaintiffs will often be able to convince a court in their home country to exercise jurisdiction over a foreign company. Yet, they find it excruciatingly difficult to enforce judgments in the foreign country where the defendant operates and has assets. Injunctions, penalties, and other sanctions cannot typically be enforced across borders. Money awards (*e.g.*, judgments for damages) may be easier to enforce, so long as they do not involve punitive or penalty elements or invoke procedural principles that offend public policy. For these and a number of practical reasons (including costs and difficulties of pursuing claims in other jurisdictions and languages), the risk of enforcement of foreign laws tends to be much lower than the risk that such laws actually apply.

Practitioners must consider a number of noteworthy exceptions, though. Companies that have contractually agreed to comply with foreign laws (*e.g.*, in the EU Standard Contractual Clauses or free-form services agreements) may be forced to comply with certain laws where their foreign business partners have the means and motivation to press the issue, for example, because they in turn are directly subject to governmental enforcement actions or consider compliance important to their business. Also, companies may have submitted to foreign laws and agreed to cooperate with foreign authorities more or less voluntarily in connection with applications for permits or licenses. Moreover, governments have powers to exclude foreign companies from national markets, *e.g.*, by blocking Internet connections directly or via orders against local telecommunications service providers.

Based on enforceability considerations, companies can create a priority list of jurisdictions whose laws are particularly likely to be enforced against them, directly or indirectly. Within this list, jurisdictions may be ranked based on the strength of connection (presence of management and key employees > incorporation and stock exchange listing > physical presence > targeted website > AI users), whether the company has contractually committed or otherwise submitted to another country's laws or jurisdiction (*e.g.*, in connection with permits or licenses), and whether the company's home jurisdiction cooperates with the foreign country on extradition and the recognition and enforcement of judgments.

If the remaining list of relevant jurisdictions is still overwhelming, companies tend to prioritize further by market considerations and turn first to countries that produce or promise substantial revenue or are known for particularly high sensitivities to AI. Aside from business concerns, you should also consider where compliance is particularly easy (*e.g.*, no language hurdles, similar legal system to your home jurisdiction). Based on such practical considerations, most companies can come up with a manageable shortlist of priority jurisdictions whose laws they address with a particular focus.

2.10   Execute

Once you have prepared a list of concrete tasks to achieve compliance and mitigate risks with respect to AI, you should start executing those tasks, focusing first on quick wins and tasks that help address particularly serious risks. Many companies find it helpful to start preparing inventories of AI as well as internal protocols and approval procedures, because in the process, they naturally try to consider all key risks and requirements. An important practical point is: don't get overwhelmed. It is better to close some compliance gaps than none. Even though many tasks are interconnected, it is often possible to complete tasks in some areas without prejudice to others, *e.g.*, mitigate risks of biased, automated decision-making concerning job applicants before or after tackling concerns regarding the integration of external AI in chatbot functionality on a consumer-facing website, and approach compliance for some priority jurisdictions before turning to others.

When you introduce brand-new requirements, consider subjecting them to an automatic expiration date and pre-scheduled review process. This is particularly important during these early days of AI law development, because you can expect an avalanche of new laws and regulations in the next few years. As they materialize, you have to refine and replace your initial measures and ideally remove and retire as many processes and documents as you add. If you only keep adding pages to your documentation and requirements for your employees and contractors, your organization will become less and less focused and your compliance program less effective over time.

3   Drafting documentation

To implement any compliance program within a company, you have to prepare documentation. Some documents you need to create because they are required by law. Other documents you may need due to operational considerations or for marketing purposes. And there are documents that people create based on recommendations or "best practices" tips that you may find upon closer examination are neither required nor helpful, but rather are liable to detract from or suffocate an organization's compliance efforts.

Before you put pen to paper, consider two threshold questions:

- Why are you creating the document?
- Who is your audience?

After you have answered these two threshold questions, you can proceed to preparing an outline. Then, consider the next two questions:

- What requirements and considerations apply regarding content, form, and organization?
- What traps and pitfalls have to be avoided?

In this chapter you will find suggestions on how to answer these threshold questions, recommendations regarding documentation that companies tend to need and not need, and guidance and considerations regarding the drafting of documents.

3.1   Why are you creating the document?

As a general matter, businesses prefer to create less rather than more documentation for a number of reasons. Chiefly, it takes resources to prepare, review, adhere to, and maintain documentation. Published documentation can limit what a company may do with respect to Artificial Intelligence (AI). Plaintiffs and regulators may exploit any failures to comply with promises and representations they find in written documentation that a company adopted but did not adhere to in practice.

Companies create AI-related documentation primarily for three reasons: laws, market demand, and organizational necessities. More specifically:

- to satisfy legal requirements or enjoy benefits that are legally conditioned on having certain documentation;
- to respond to market demand (for example, from customers, suppliers, investors, or employees); and
- to communicate and memorialize rules, instructions, and restrictions internally within the organization to ensure that employees do the right thing.

Sometimes, it can be possible and most effective to pursue more than one of these three objectives within the same document. But, usually it is best to create separate documents for each purpose, and it is always important to determine and focus on your particular objective(s). We look at some of these objectives in the next sections.

3.1.1   Legal purposes

If you are trying to satisfy a particular legal requirement, you should first carefully analyze its source, applicability, and elements. For example, companies that collect any data online from consumers in California for their own purposes have to post a website privacy policy according to the California Online Privacy Protection Act of 2003 (CalOPPA) and other laws around the world modeled after it. Under the EU General Data Protection Regulation (GDPR) and since 2023 under the California Consumer Privacy Act (CCPA), even businesses that sell only to other businesses have to post privacy notices. Yet, under these and most other privacy laws, companies do not have to disclose their practices concerning personal data they process on behalf of enterprise customers as a "processor" (in GDPR-speak) or as a "service provider" (in CCPA-speak). In this respect, only the customer is required to inform the data subjects. This is appropriate, because the customer is the one that determines purposes and means of personal data processing as a "controller" (in GDPR-speak) or "business" (in CCPA-speak). Nevertheless, some AI providers also explain their business services offerings in their website privacy policies.

Some companies find it helpful in customer contract negotiations if they can incorporate into services agreements the service descriptions published in their website privacy policies. Customers may be more reasonable about demanding changes concerning details in published privacy policies, because customers know how difficult it is to change their own privacy policy. But, service providers should carefully consider pros and cons of this approach. They could expose themselves to expectations from data subjects and regulators to take more responsibility for processing activities if they implicitly hold themselves out as "controllers." Also, regulators may complain that required privacy notices have become too long if companies add topics and details that they are not required to cover by law. If companies decide to address topics in website privacy statements voluntarily, they should be cognizant of the fact that they are not legally required to do so and also weigh potential disadvantages.

Similarly, you should consult the relevant legislative text whenever you are creating documentation to ensure you benefit from the advantages that are conditioned on having such documentation. For example, under the GDPR, companies are required to provide job candidates, consumers, and other data subjects a right to object to automated decision-making if the decision produces legal effects or similarly significantly affects the data subject. If you are trying to satisfy such a legal requirement, you should re-read the legislative text to assess whether your process qualifies as automated decision-making (which may or may not require the deployment of AI) and whether the impact of your decision rises to the level of a legal or similarly significant effect. Then you can assess whether the burden and disadvantages of compliance (*e.g.*, offering a right to object) might frustrate or outweigh the benefits of the planned activity (*e.g.*, automating job application scanning). Sometimes the available benefits may not be worth the hassle.

Companies are not typically required under privacy laws to extend an express promise in a privacy policy never to share customer data. Some companies expect that more consumers will grant consent in consideration for voluntary promises. Other companies believe that most consumers do not read or appreciate privacy notices at all. If a company extends a promise not to share data, this can severely limit the value of its databases with respect to potential future business models as well as in merger and acquisition (M&A) situations or bankruptcy.

With respect to the sources of notice and consent requirements, companies should not merely consider statutory law but also contractual obligations that they may have assumed in dealing with business partners or the data subjects themselves. For example, companies that committed in public privacy policies to notify data subjects by email at least 30 days before they change their privacy policy have to honor such promises, even though they may not have been legally required to extend such promises in the first place.

3.1.2   Business purposes

When you are trying to address business needs, you should clearly formulate (or ask other stakeholders in the company to formulate) the exact objectives, the expected negative consequences from satisfying versus not satisfying the demands, and how the company will benefit. Even if you do not have much time and resources to dig in deep, you should at least make a rudimentary assessment of the perceived benefits and burdens. Too often, companies seem to copy language from competitors or perceived industry trendsetters without closely analyzing why other companies chose the particular language and without assessing the pros and cons of adopting templates for their own business. In lieu of thoughtful analysis, the term "best practices" tends to be (ab)used to justify following examples of other companies that may be in a completely different situation. For example, consumer-facing AI providers face different expectations depending on whether they offer access to AI free of charge or via paid subscription. Consumers who pay for a subscription may expect more robust security standards and protection of their input and output.

Also, consumers may expect better data protection from an AI chatbot on their physician's site than from a general-purpose AI chatbot that an online retailer deploys to handle returns. AI providers can also expect greatly varying levels of scrutiny depending on whether they target private start-up companies, large multinationals, public sector entities, or regulated industries. All companies tend to be affected to some degree by their competitors and any industry-wide practices. You have to gather some information about customer expectations and common industry practices before you can effectively tailor documents to pursue a market-driven agenda.

You should be conscious of the minimum requirements you have or want to satisfy and whether going above and beyond is rewarded in any respect. You could expose your business to unreasonable degrees of risk if you advertise a Large Language Model (LLM) that generates output based on probabilistic methods as a source of truthful information instead of a generator of draft text that users must review and validate before relying on its factual accuracy. More broadly, you should avoid adding "marketing fluff" to any documents other than advertisements. For example, privacy professionals often include statements about having extraordinary respect for consumer privacy or deploying state-of-the art security technologies in privacy policies, but such statements are neither required by law nor readily substantiated. Companies rarely benefit from such statements and regularly find that these assertions are used against them by regulators and plaintiffs.

3.1.3   Organizational purposes

If you are creating documentation to communicate instructions within the organization for operational reasons, carefully consider and define the addressees of your instructions. Many companies have started to implement lengthy AI policies, addressed to anyone and no one, covering a whole array of topics from high-level ethical principles, diversity and inclusion objectives, data acquisition for AI training, automated decision-making, privacy rights, and the installation of software updates. Individual employees are unlikely to read or remember all the details of such unwieldy documents. An employee can be better reached with short, pointed protocols addressed to particular departments or groups of employees, ideally presented in places and at times as close as possible to the moment when the employee should follow the particular instruction.

Employees should be reminded that they must not submit confidential information or sensitive personal data outside non-disclosure and data processing agreements when they visit publicly available AI offerings or Internet search engines. Warnings regarding network security should pop up when system users connect private devices or access the company's network remotely. When a manager is prompted to draft a business plan or staff evaluation, an alert regarding the company's AI chatbot use restrictions may be in order. Rules on shredding confidential printouts are best attached to printers in the office.

When you create protocols, also consider what kinds of rules you can realistically expect people to follow. Companies that disseminate protocols that ultimately are not followed can subject themselves to claims from employees and others who assert that they relied on the safeguards contemplated in the protocols. Also, regulators and private plaintiffs could use the fact that a company adopted a protocol but did not follow it as evidence that the company acknowledged a certain duty of care and then negligently violated it. To reduce such risks, you can add disclaimers to protocols according to which the document should not be relied on, is not intended to create third party beneficiary rights or privacy expectations, and contains only internal instructions, as suggested in the examples contained in Chapter 6 of this Field Guide. But, it is even more important to create narrower protocols that can and will be followed.

3.2   Who is your audience?

After you answer the big "why" question, you should identify your audience. With a particular audience in mind, you can pick appropriate language and style, assess which details you have to explain or can presume are known, and decide which points to highlight.

For example, if you are addressing regulators or attorneys, you want to be precise and follow statutory terminology as much as possible. You should have the text of the particular statute or other source of law right in front of you when you draft your document, to identify the minimum requirements as to content, organization, terminology, form, and delivery. You can presume that your reader knows, or can access and understand, the law, and you should focus on facts and circumstances relevant to your particular situation. If you organize your document by following specific statutory requirements and terminology in the order they appear in the statute, you help your reader check off each compliance requirement. This way, you can optimize the effect of your document.

On the other hand, if you are writing to consumers or employees outside the legal department, you may have to lead with some basic explanations and use everyday language to get your message across. In an agreement covering the use of application program interfaces (API) to an AI offering, you may refer to "Customer" and "Supplier" as defined terms, but in website terms of use concerning the same AI functionality, you may prefer to write about "you" and "us."

If you are drafting documentation to meet marketing demands or communicate instructions to employees regarding data processing and privacy-related matters, you should tailor the content, organization, terminology, form, and delivery of your notice to the particular needs at hand. You should start with points that are particularly important and least likely to be already known by your particular audience, use terminology that the audience is familiar with, and present your document at a place and time when it is most likely to have its intended effect. For example, if you want to induce prospective customers to choose your AI products or services because of superior accuracy or safety features, you should tout such features in advertisements, product descriptions, and other text that prospects read when they make their purchasing decisions. Privacy statements or services terms are less suited for advertising purposes. Most consumers do not read privacy statements or terms of service. Plaintiffs' counsel and regulators do, however, and they tend to use any promotional touting against the company. Also, if you want employees to follow company rules about using AI, you should consider using pop-up screens on computers rather than burying notices in wordy policy statements, standard contract terms, or thick employee handbooks. You may be able to refer to inconspicuously presented notices to support disciplinary actions, but they tend to do little to prevent offenses in the first place. So, think about where, when, and how best to get your intended message across to your audience, and consider all options that old and new media offer, including real-time pop-up screens, video and audio prompts, interactive quizzes, and warning signs.

To serve the document's purpose efficiently, it can be helpful to use the title itself to indicate to whom the document is addressed. If you find an "AI policy" in your company that is not addressed to a particular audience, ask whether its purpose is to direct employees on how to develop or use AI, notify the public about your company's code of conduct concerning AI use, or disclose automated decision-making to potentially affected data subjects. If you cannot determine the purpose or audience from reading the title of the document, chances are that you do not need it.

3.3   Differentiate categories of documentation

Most organizations will need the following categories of documentation for purposes of complying with AI laws.

- **Legal memos** are documents in which attorneys explain compliance requirements, claims, and defenses. Clients can refuse to disclose legal memos to authorities under subpoenas and to plaintiffs in court cases if the clients keep them confidential and under attorney–client privilege. Most jurisdictions recognize such a privilege to enable clients to communicate openly with legal counsel, which increases chances that they can understand and comply with applicable laws. To preserve the privilege, clients have to keep communications confidential. In Germany and some other jurisdictions, they may have to keep memos off the premises with their outside counsel to remove the documents from the grip of authorities during dawn raids, *i.e.*, unannounced inspection and seizure operations at European subsidiaries of multinationals headquartered in the United States, which European authorities often conduct in the early morning, when the executives and in-house counsels in the United States are still asleep. If European authorities find memos with confidential legal advice on the premises of a company, they often confiscate the documents and ignore objections based on attorney–client privilege.
- **Impact, compliance, and risk assessments** are documents in which companies explain how they comply with applicable law. While you are working on a risk assessment, you should try to keep it confidential and under attorney–client privilege, like a legal memo. But, once you finalize the assessment, you should keep it for the specific purpose of disclosing it to authorities in cases of audits or lawsuits as evidence of your due diligence and adherence to standards of care.
- **Notices**, including alerts and warnings, are documents in which companies communicate important facts or legally required disclosures externally, for example, to alert consumers that they are communicating with an AI chatbot, job applicants that their resumés are screened by AI tools, or airline passengers that they are being authenticated by facial recognition systems. Notices primarily serve legal purposes and their audiences are persons who are potentially affected by AI.
- **Consent forms**, including licenses and releases, are documents with which companies seek permission, for example, to utilize user prompts and feedback for continuing AI training. Consent forms

primarily serve legal purposes. Their audiences can be individuals or legal entities whose consent is required under applicable laws.

- **Agreements**, including disclaimers and license agreements, are documents with which companies create or modify rights and obligations regarding AI, for example, disclaimers regarding AI accuracy to limit liability, copyright license agreements with book publishers for training data, data acquisition services agreements with contractors to scrape training data from public websites, and services agreements between developers, providers, and users of AI. Some agreements exclusively serve legal compliance purposes (*e.g.*, business associate agreements under HIPAA with hospitals that want to deploy AI to help answer patient queries, or data processing agreements under the GDPR); others serve business purposes (*e.g.*, online user agreements). The agreement's audience can be individual users, corporate users, or AI providers, or individual employees as contracting parties, *e.g.*, in the context of employee inventions agreements or data security undertakings.
- **Protocols** contain instructions on how to develop, provide, or use AI. Protocols usually serve organizational needs and their audience usually consists of employees and contractors.
- **Data submission forms** are documents with which companies allow or solicit the submission of information, for example, data subject requests and consumer feedback. Companies use surveys, job candidate questionnaires, registration pages, and web forms where people can specify communication preferences or lodge complaints regarding infringements. Such forms can serve legal, marketing, and organizational purposes, and their audiences vary accordingly.

Companies, legislatures, and regulators use different terminology for documentation. Specifically, you can find the term "policy" used in reference to notices (*e.g.*, website privacy policy), protocols (*e.g.*, investigation processes), and policy statements (*e.g.*, memorializing an approach to compliance the organization decided to take). Particularly with respect to policies, it sometimes seems that drafters are confused about purpose and audience. Within larger organizations, you often find a mix of aspirational marketing fluff, internal instructions, and external notifications in documents labeled "AI policies." No particular audience or purpose is effectively served by such multi-purpose documents. If you are not sure what to call a particular document, consider whether a law, industry practice, or audience expectation favors one label over another. In the absence of other compelling considerations, it is probably best to use the term prescribed in the law you are trying to comply with. For example, California law requires a "website privacy policy" and "privacy notices," each for purposes of informing data subjects what you do with their data. Whatever label you end up using, you should make sure that titles or labels do not obscure the purpose or audience of the document.

Every company has different needs for documentation. You may not need all of the documents in the following table and you may need additional documents. But, if you are just getting started, it may be helpful to ask yourself whether your company has or needs some or all of the following documents.

Table 3.1   *Sample documentation categories*

Category	Title	Addressees	Primary Purpose
Legal memos	AI Compliance Requirements	Management, decision-makers	Enabling compliance
Notices	Website Privacy Statement	Website visitors	Satisfying legal notice requirements
	DMCA (Digital Millennium Copyright Act) Notice	Copyright owners	Qualifying for privileges concerning contributory liability for infringement by AI users
	Alerts regarding automated decision-making	Subjects of automated decisions, *e.g.,* job applicants	Satisfying legal notice requirements

Category	Title	Addressees	Primary Purpose
	Employee Privacy Notices regarding employee files, computer monitoring, whistleblower hotlines	Employees	Satisfying legal notice requirements (*e.g.*, in Europe, California) or negating privacy expectations (*e.g.*, in other U.S. states)
	Data Security Breach Notification	Customers, employees, regulators	Satisfying legal notice requirements, mitigating damages
Consent forms	Informed Consent to AI Testing Project	Study participants	Compliance with Common Rule, laws on human subject research
	Use of prompts for AI training	AI users	Satisfying legal requirements or addressing customer expectations
	Copyright licenses or release forms	Training data providers	Satisfying legal requirements
Agreements	AI development and use agreements	Developers, providers, users	Defining commercial terms
	Website terms of use	Website visitors	Granting or denying access to web crawlers and other scraping tools for purposes of acquiring training data

Category	Title	Addressees	Primary Purpose
	Confidentiality / Data Security Agreements	Individual independent contractors, employees	Keeping personal data secure; securing remedies under contracts and trade secret law; asserting proprietary rights to data; satisfying compliance obligations
	Descriptions of technical and organizational data security measures (TOMs)	Suppliers, customers	Complying with legal requirements on data processing agreements; defining data security measures and limitations
	Data transfer and processing agreements based on Standard Contractual Clauses, HIPAA, Payment Card Industry (PCI) standards	Processors	Keeping personal data secure; complying with restrictions on international data transfers from the EEA
	Appointment of Data Protection Officer (DPO)	DPO	Satisfying legal requirements; defining term, role, rights, duties, and limitations
Protocols	AI Use Protocol	All employees	Operational, *e.g.*, limiting use cases, submission of personal data in prompts

Category	Title	Addressees	Primary Purpose
	Information Security Protocol	IT department	Defining security measures, technologies, and processes; meeting statutory obligations
	Data Acquisition Protocol	Developers	Defining limits and precautions for scraping and other data acquisition
	External Code Usage Protocol	Programmers	Instructions on compliance with open source license terms, use of AI to write code, due diligence
	Data Retention Protocol	IT department and user groups	Defining minimum / maximum data retention periods
	Direct Marketing Protocol	Sales and marketing department	Complying with anti-spam laws
Data submission forms	Data Subject Requests for Data Access, Correction, Deletion	Data subjects	Complying with law; channeling requests
	Fields for chatbot prompts, feedback, or search engines	Users	Soliciting user input
	Complaint form for copyright infringement or content concerns	Users, third parties	Risk mitigation concerning third party claims
	Online account registration form	Consumers, employees	User authentication

Category	Title	Addressees	Primary Purpose
Descriptions	Risk assessments	Legal department, regulators	Obtain or provide legal advice; demonstrate compliance to regulators
	Compliance dossier	Data protection authorities	Compliance with law (*e.g.*, Art. 5.2 GDPR, California Age-Appropriate Design Code Act (CAADCA)) or compliance program management
	Technical and organizational data security measures (TOMs)	Corporate customers of data processing services	Defining contractual standard for required security measures; satisfying market demands on service providers

3.4 Legal advice, risks, and compliance efforts

While you are exploring legal requirements or responding to a lawsuit, you should keep legal advice confidential and under attorney–client privilege. While you work on draft AI compliance documentation, you will inevitably explore risks and mitigation measures that your company will not ultimately pursue, due to time pressures and resource limitations. You will be more effective at addressing all risks if you document them in writing as a basis for obtaining legal advice. But, to foster frank and open communications, you should keep initial discussions confidential and privileged. If risks materialize, plaintiffs and regulators could cite unprivileged documentation against your company, potentially unfairly and out of context. Therefore, you should carefully draw lines between (1) confidential and privileged risk assessments and legal advice on the one hand, and (2) compliance documentation that you want to produce in defense of your decisions and compliance program, on the other.

3.4.1   Attorney-client privilege

In order to preserve privilege, you have to meet different requirements, which vary from jurisdiction to jurisdiction. In general, you have to ensure that you communicate about legal advice with attorneys who are licensed in the jurisdiction where you may need to claim privilege and that you do not share the communications with persons who do not need to know. Courts and authorities in the United States tend to respect adequately marked and protected documents as covered by privilege, but authorities in Europe and other jurisdictions may confiscate even privileged documents in dawn raids if companies keep them on their premises. Therefore, multinational businesses need to carefully decide whom to involve in the preparation and delivery of legal advice on sensitive topics and where they physically keep legal memos.

If you are working on a response to a cybersecurity incident, an investigation, or a lawsuit, you should prioritize privilege considerations. Also, at the outset of developing an AI law compliance program and processes, you should take attorney–client privilege considerations into account. Later, as you proceed to implementation of your compliance program, you will have to balance confidentiality considerations with the need to get things done.

In Chapter 4 you will find more information on risks and mitigation measures that you should consider specifically in the context of AI impact assessments.

3.4.2   Documentation to demonstrate compliance

After you provide or obtain legal advice under privilege, you should proceed to preparing documentation that you can use to demonstrate compliance in response to customer inquiries, audits, requests for information from authorities, subpoenas, and discovery motions from plaintiffs in class action lawsuits. While you are working with attorneys, you should keep drafts under privilege and apply strict confidentiality measures.

Companies are required to demonstrate compliance under a number of laws pertaining to AI, including the GDPR and New York City's Local Law 144 of 2021 regarding automated employment decision tools ("AEDT"). Companies also prepare compliance documentation in response to customer inquiries and due diligence information request lists in M&A transactions, and to defend against possible future charges of negligence in litigation. Such descriptive documents are also helpful in conducting a legal review of existing or planned practices, *e.g.*, regarding plans to offer an AI product or service to users in other jurisdictions.

To prepare such documentation, you could identify and expressly list the requirements that you are addressing and then describe next to each requirement what your company is actually doing. For example, you could copy and paste each GDPR principle and key obligations for AI under other laws into a blank document, divided by page breaks, and then add company-specific information on how the company addresses each requirement. Before you finalize or share the documentation, make sure that the efforts described are accurate and sufficient (or change your practices) and that they are consistent with your representations to users (in product specifications, terms, privacy notices, or advertisements), government authorities (in filings), business partners (in contracts), and others. Even smaller organizations usually benefit from creating a compliance dossier to collect and monitor all of their various compliance tasks and measures (such as copyright clearance, licenses, privacy notices, filings, appointments of Data Protection Officers (DPOs), data transfer agreements, and policies). This will also help ensure that the information communicated to authorities is consistent.

Audit and consulting firms often recommend that companies start compliance projects with a gap assessment, to identify specific compliance deficits that require remediation. Companies with mature compliance programs can benefit from this approach. But, often companies end up with voluminous reports that flag significant problems but that may not be protected by attorney–client privilege. If they fail to remedy deficits identified in such reports quickly, they have increased their risks and liabilities by ordering the gap assessment, and the project becomes counterproductive. In the run-up to GDPR and CCPA compliance deadlines, many smaller and less advanced organizations spent disproportionate amounts of time, resources, and budgets on formal gap assessments, instead of incrementally addressing new requirements and known deficits. Generally, companies should first focus on addressing compliance requirements and documenting positive compliance measures in a dossier, before they turn to audits and gap assessments.

Under the GDPR, companies are specifically required to conduct and document data protection impact assessments (DPIAs) and consult their DPO before they implement new data processing technologies or processes that are likely to result in high risk to data subjects. If a controller determines that a proposed technology or process would result in high risk, then it must consult with data protection authorities. The authorities can hardly be expected to approve a high-risk proposal. Therefore, in practice, companies conduct DPIAs to determine how they can mitigate risks sufficiently, and to document why they decide to proceed without consulting authorities.

In the United States and Canada, government agencies have already been obligated since the early 2000s to conduct privacy impact assessments. Also, many technology companies have required privacy impact assessments for years as part of their product development process to determine the legality of intended product use cases, risks of direct or contributory liability for product misuse, and ultimately the chances of commercial success. With respect to AI, these topics could be addressed within a broader AI risk assessment. But, where consultation with a DPO or authority is required, companies may prefer to create a stand-alone version of statutorily required DPIA documentation to streamline any review focused on personal data protection.

Whether or not a specific statutory requirement applies, companies should assess the impact of new products and processes on individual privacy, security, and other rights and interests, and document risk mitigation measures during design and implementation. Companies can use the resulting documentation to develop "privacy by design" guidance for developers, refine product and services specifications, draft user instructions, answer questions from prospective customers regarding legal and responsible product adoption, defend against claims based on contributory liability theories in cases of product abuse, and demonstrate accountability in case of audits or challenges by data or consumer protection authorities.

In a DPIA document, companies should describe at a minimum:

- how the new product, service, or process works;
- categories of data, subjects, controllers, processors, suppliers, and recipients involved;
- processing operations, purposes of the data processing, and interests of the controller;
- potential risks for data subjects;
- risk mitigation measures designed into the product, service, or process, including the measures envisaged to address the risks, such as safeguards, security measures, and mechanisms to ensure the protection of personal data and to demonstrate compliance, taking into account the rights and legitimate interests of data subjects and other persons concerned;
- risk mitigation measures that users can apply;
- notices and choices provided to data subjects;
- assessment of the necessity and proportionality of the processing operations in relation to the purposes;
- balancing of interests of controllers versus data subjects; and
- an overall conclusion regarding the justification of the proposed data processing.

In the interest of efficiency, try to cover similar products, services, and processes in one DPIA, and keep documents short and concise. Companies can benefit more from a few thoughtful and actionable one-pagers covering all high-risk aspects of their business than from numerous complex and lengthy assessments. Also, legal counsel and DPOs can advise more quickly and effectively on privacy law questions if you approach them with a precise statement of facts required for a data protection impact assessment.

3.5   Notices

When you start preparing or reviewing documentation for a compliance program, you will find more prescriptive requirements for notices than for other documents, and particular attention to detail is important for a number of reasons:

- You will find notice requirements as a minimum standard in most draft bills concerning AI and already in effect concerning automated decision-making (GDPR) and chatbot disclosure requirements (California law). You will soon need additional notices everywhere.

- If you do not publish notices as required, data subjects and regulators detect omissions and deficiencies relatively quickly and complain.
- Notices are a condition and building block for consent. Without an adequate notice, a study participant or data subject cannot grant informed consent.

What exactly you have to disclose in a privacy notice depends on the particular legal requirement you are trying to satisfy. Some companies describe in their website privacy statements particulars of AI offerings or data processing services that they sell to corporate customers. For example, companies that offer AI on a Software-as-a-Service (SaaS) basis to business customers may describe in their website privacy statement not only how they collect data from website visitors, but also how their enterprise service works and what data security measures they have implemented. This is usually not required and often not appropriate. With respect to the enterprise services, the provider is a mere processor of personal data. Its customer, as the controller, is obligated to notify the individual data subjects (*e.g.*, the customer's employees or consumers). If a service provider nevertheless addresses notices directly to the customer's employees, customers, or other data subjects, the provider achieves no legal compliance requirement and can suffer a number of adverse consequences, including that the service provider may:

- create the impression that the provider is responsible as controller (*e.g.*, for data access and correction purposes – which the provider cannot possibly live up to without violating its customer contracts);
- expose itself to direct liability vis-à-vis data subjects;
- contradict the customer's own notices (which could result in confusion and corresponding liability);
- lock itself into particular limitations, which can prevent the provider from accommodating customer requests regarding customization.

Companies that use AI should not leave it entirely to their service providers to issue notices. The company that uses AI for its own purposes should be the one to issue appropriate notices and include information about data processing activities performed by vendors. Vendors need to supply technical details to customers, and they can help their customers prepare factually correct and comprehensive notices, but the customer, as controller, needs to ensure via contracts and audits that vendor activities comply with the customer's representations in its own notices.

3.6   Warnings

Warnings are a particularly focused type of notice. With a warning, companies can draw attention to particular risks. AI providers should consider warning users of particular dangers, *e.g.*, that AI output may be inaccurate or that users should not include sensitive personal information in prompts. With conspicuous alerts, AI providers can reduce the risks of harm to users and third parties, and indirectly reduce their own potential liability if harm nevertheless materializes.

You have to phrase warnings concisely and present them conspicuously at the place and time the person you are addressing can act to avoid the danger. Companies that bury warnings in lengthy privacy notices or terms of use may be able to refer to the warning in the context of a legal dispute, but they will likely not prevent harm. Few employees, consumers, and others read lengthy documents.

An AI chatbot provider could design a prompt filter that triggers a warning if an AI user submits personal health information. The provider could include the warning in the chatbot response or present a separate pop-up box with an alert along the following lines, "Remember, never include sensitive personal information in prompts. Read our Terms of Use and Privacy Notice" [hyperlink to the Terms of Use and Privacy Notice]. Some AI providers already configure their chatbots to warn users in conversations that they are not licensed to provide legal advice, that the training data does not cover current events, and that users must verify output before they rely on it or disseminate it as factual information.

3.7   Consent

Some laws prescribe that one has to obtain consent before engaging in certain types of activities. When people seek or grant consent, they also refer to consent as acceptance, agreement, approval, assent, authorization, license, or permission. For example, under the Computer Fraud and Abuse Act (CFAA), no one may access a computer to obtain information for AI training purposes without or exceeding the computer owner's authorization, including from web servers via sites whose terms of use expressly prohibit scraping. Under copyright law, one must not reproduce copyrighted works for AI training purposes without a license from the copyright owner. A business must not use an individual's name, likeness, or identity to advertise an AI product or service unless the individual consents. Under U.S. federal law (namely the HIPAA privacy rule), hospitals have to obtain certain qualified authorizations from patients if they want to use personal health information outside the scope of statutory permissions. Under the Common Rule and EU regulations on clinical trials, companies may have to obtain informed consent from individual study participants and permission from ethics committees or institutional review boards before they conduct clinical trials and other human subject research. Under European data protection laws, companies have to seek prior consent before they send promotional emails or place cookies on consumers' computers, except with consent.

3.7.1   Required, beneficial, and optional consent

Besides situations where consent is absolutely required or absolutely insufficient, companies frequently find they have to decide whether they could and should obtain consent. For example, under European data protection laws, companies have the option to obtain consent from data subjects to use personal data in AI user prompts for training purposes to overcome the general prohibition of automated data processing. As an alternative to seeking consent, companies can also conclude contracts with data subjects that require the processing, or determine whether they can rely on an overriding legitimate interest where permitted under applicable law. In practice, it can be unclear whether such alternative justifications are truly available. The balancing of interests involves a fair amount of discretion and one can also argue whether certain processing arrangements are truly "necessary" under a contract. Therefore, companies often consider whether they should perhaps seek consent "just in case." Also, under the laws of many countries that have not (yet) enacted specific data privacy or data protection laws, local attorneys often recommend seeking consent from data subjects to protect against the risk of challenges mounted based on general tort statutes or vague constitutional principles.

Before you decide to seek consent "just in case," however, you should answer the following questions:

*   Do any laws restrict the validity, effect, or scope of consent, or establish burdensome formal or substantive conditions? If you are dealing with children, for example, you may have to seek parental consent separately.
*   How easy is it to obtain and keep track of consent? An online retailer can obtain consent relatively easily from online shoppers in the context of online account registrations and purchase processes, although each time the seller requires buyers to make a decision and confirm it via a separate click, this creates friction and deters some consumers, reducing the number of completed transactions. An online researcher who accesses websites to download content to generate AI training sets, on the other hand, finds it much more difficult, if not impractical, to obtain consent for scraping from website operators. If it is too difficult to obtain valid consent, you may be better off not asking, unless you absolutely and clearly need consent.
*   Are any government authorities, works councils, union leadership, or other institutions opposed to your seeking consent? For example, data protection authorities, consumer protection associations, and collective employee representatives tend to be skeptical of companies that seek consent for data usage in the context of unrelated processes, and they quickly complain about coercion or dark patterns, *i.e.*, methods intended to manipulate a person into consenting. In the employment context, many European data protection authorities presume employee consent to be invalid, and so companies need to consider other compliance approaches to avoid confrontation with the authorities.
*   Is there a risk of disrupting an existing business relationship by seeking consent? Often, if you ask something of an employee, consumer, or business partner, they expect something in return. If you are offering a benefit and your request for consent is legitimately related to that benefit, you will usually be able to secure consent easily (*e.g.*, if you offer customization of AI chatbot functionality in consideration for permission to use prompts and feedback for training purposes). But, obtaining consent may be more difficult when you are seeking consent to an activity that does not benefit the data subject and perhaps even affects the data subject adversely (*e.g.*, employee

monitoring for security purposes). Thus, consider what you can offer to induce data subjects to grant consent voluntarily.

- What can you do and what will you do if your request for consent is denied? If you have to proceed anyhow, then seeking consent may not be an appropriate option, unless you can do business and are content to do business only with those who consent.

- What can you do and what will you do if you receive consent initially, but later consent is revoked? If this is not acceptable, you may have to look for compliance approaches that do not require you to obtain consent in the first place. Under most European data protection laws, data subjects remain free to revoke consent. Under copyright laws, however, copyright owners can generally grant irrevocable licenses. Also, you try to discourage consent revocation by providing for adverse consequences in agreements, for example, by contractually holding data subjects responsible to pay for any business disruption, losses, and costs resulting from consent revocation. Yet, it is often questionable whether such agreements are enforceable against employees or consumers based on doctrines such as unconscionability and contracts of adhesion.

- Are you prepared to seek consent to changes when you need to expand or modify the scope of consent? If you seek consent in situations where you do not have to, you are creating actual expectations and perhaps even contractual entitlements to come back and ask for consent again before you make any changes in the future.

- Are you invoking additional legal regimes, scrutiny, and jurisdiction by seeking consent? German consumer protection watchdogs can take action against unfair contract terms under German national law, for example, including in license terms and privacy statements that are referenced in consent declarations.

3.7.2   How to obtain valid consent

If a company decides to seek consent, it has to determine the legal requirements for that consent. For example, a copyright owner can grant consent with licenses that are exclusive or non-exclusive, royalty-bearing or free, revocable or irrevocable, personal or assignable, and pertain to different territories and activities. Under European data protection laws, consent is valid only if it constitutes a "freely given, specific and informed indication of his wishes by which the data subject signifies his agreement to personal data relating to him being processed." If it concerns "special categories of personal data" (*i.e.*, "sensitive personal data"), the consent must also be "explicit." If international transfers outside the EEA are contemplated, consent must additionally be "unambiguous."

When you determine the applicable requirements, look for the following attributes in the applicable statute or contracts:

- *Prior*: consent laws usually imply that companies have to obtain consent before they do whatever it is that requires consent, but some laws expressly state that "prior consent" is needed.
- *Informed*: typically, the consenting party has to receive sufficient information to allow an informed decision, *e.g.*, in a privacy notice or detailed license agreement.
- *In writing*: some laws require handwritten or qualified digital signatures or even witnesses and notarization; for example, under a California privacy law from 1981, the Confidentiality of Medical Information Act, companies must obtain consent in handwriting or typeface no smaller than 14-point type. In the absence of specific form requirements, however, consent can be obtained verbally or electronically – the latter usually being preferable for evidentiary reasons.
- *Voluntary*: some laws specifically state that consent is valid only if the data subject agrees voluntarily; even where voluntariness is not specifically called out as a condition in the applicable law, most laws would not recognize coerced declarations as valid. A key question, then, is what negative consequences will a person suffer as a consequence of denying or revoking consent and whether the resulting pressure renders the consent invalid; for example, patients in a hospital or employees during their probationary period tend to be under more significant pressures than online gaming fans. To mitigate against the risk that consent is found involuntary (and hence invalid), companies should clearly inform the data subject of the consequences of denying or revoking consent and make a judgment call as to whether such consequences are unnecessarily harsh and could be mitigated (*e.g.*, by offering alternative business models, services, or prices for non-consenting data subjects).
- *Express, explicit, affirmative, unambiguous, and similar attributes*: these criteria apply to the actions required of the consenting party when consent is obtained. For example, a consumer might be deemed to consent impliedly by proceeding with a registration without unchecking pre-checked boxes or by failing to respond to a prompt.

Yet, such inaction will not usually satisfy requirements that consent be express, explicit, affirmative, or unambiguous. To satisfy these requirements, companies may have to require that the consenting person sign a declaration, click on a button, tick an unchecked box, or otherwise take more active steps to declare consent.

• *Specific and similar attributes*: these requirements can relate to the scope of the consent (which can be limited to particularly identified controllers, subjects, categories, and processing purposes, or be broad and unspecific) or to the focus of the document with which a company obtains consent (which can be limited to data processing or also cover various contract terms, program benefits, technology features, or use recommendations). For example, if an online merchant offers a consumer a 10 percent discount on a sale if the consumer accepts a new credit card from a particular credit card company, the consumer can grant specific consent to the one-time transfer of personal data to the credit card company for a particular purpose. By contrast, if an online merchant asks the consumer for consent to receive "valuable offers from trusted business partners," the frequency of disclosures, identities of data recipients, and purposes of data processing are less clearly defined and the resulting consent is therefore less specific.

• *Separate or distinguishable*: some laws (including HIPAA and the Fair Credit Reporting Act in the United States) require that companies obtain consent on separate documents, not combined with other declarations, so that the data subject is made particularly aware of the importance of consent to data processing; under the GDPR, companies must present requests for consent in a clearly distinguishable, intelligible, and easily accessible form, using clear and plain language.

3.7.3   Opt in, opt out, and in between

Consumers, employees, and most other individuals rarely formulate or otherwise shape the scope or terms of consent themselves. Usually, companies and governments prepare standard consent declarations and prompt individuals to declare consent in a prescribed form and process to allow uniform data processing practices and easy confirmation of whether consent has been granted. If you do not obtain consent through pre-formulated forms, but rather via online chats or email exchanges, you will inevitably face challenges regarding the interpretation and documentation of consent.

Examples of consent mechanisms. Before you settle on a particular approach, you should consider applicable legal requirements and the many different practical ways data subjects can declare consent, including the following options arranged here roughly in descending order of explicitness:

(a)   by signing their name on a paper form specifically relating to data processing;

(b)   by checking two unchecked boxes on an online form specifically relating to data processing, one where the data subjects declare that they have understood the scope of the consent, and another where the data subjects declare that they wish to consent (*a.k.a.* the "French double-click process");

(c)   by checking an unchecked box and then responding to an email that is automatically sent after an online registration and consent process to expressly confirm that the data subjects have read and understood the request and want to consent (*a.k.a.* the "German double opt-in process");

(d)   by checking an unchecked box on an online form specifically allowing an AI provider to use prompts and feedback for AI training;

(e)   by replying "yes" after being asked about call monitoring or recording during an online chat or phone conversation;

(f)   by signing their name or checking an unchecked box to agree to a set of contract terms that include a pre-formulated consent declaration (for example, in an online banking services agreement, autonomous car rental agreement, or terms of use regarding a charge-free website). Implementations vary in many ways, such as:

   (i)   Consumers can be presented with a consent declaration with a separate heading in CAPITAL LETTERS or **bold print** within a larger document, at the beginning or end of the larger document, to meet requirements under the GDPR and other laws providing that consent requests be clearly distinguishable from other terms; but, in practice, it is not uncommon for consent declarations to be included somewhere in the middle of legal terms, without any special formatting that would catch the data subject's eyes;

   (ii)   The document containing the consent declaration can be presented:

      1.   in a separate window that website visitors have to scroll through before they can proceed;

2. on the same page – beneath or above an "agree" or "consent" button;

3. on a separate web page, which the data subject can access by clicking on a hyperlink that is placed above or beneath a consent button; or

4. on a separate web page that is linked on the bottom of the page via a general text link "data privacy" or just "legal," unrelated to the website portions with which visitors interact to declare consent.

(g) by proceeding with an online registration or other process without unchecking a pre-checked box presented on a web page;

(h) by proceeding with an online registration or other process after having received a notice (*e.g.*, a link to a privacy statement) according to which the individual can opt out of automated decision-making or certain data processing activities such as profiling or email marketing (*e.g.*, by re-configuring "communication preference" settings in an online account or sending an unsubscribe request);

(i) by proceeding with an online chat or phone call after receiving notice that it is possible to request that the call not be "recorded or monitored for quality control or training";

(j) by not taking any action after receiving a just-in-time, specific, and conspicuous notice that the data subject is able to opt out of certain data processing (*e.g.*, automated decision-making); or

(k) by not taking any action after receiving a one-time or annual notice that the data subject is able to opt out of certain data processing activities.

In all of the aforementioned scenarios, a person arguably declares consent. Thus, any of these alternatives may be sufficient if a law simply requires consent without specifying any additional attributes of the consent. But, you should consider a number of additional factors to determine whether you are able to secure consent as required by law in particular scenarios:

Before or after contract formation. An important factor applicable to all previous scenarios is whether a company prompts the data subject with a consent request before entering into a relationship (*e.g.*, in the context of enrollment in a new online service or online job application) or after concluding a contract (*e.g.*, a prompt for consent declaration pops up during the installation of software that the data subject previously purchased in a store; or an employer requests an employee to agree to workplace surveillance after signing an employment contract). Before a contract is concluded, actions or omissions can imply that an individual assents to terms that a company unilaterally presents if the individual gains a benefit that the company is not required to grant (*e.g.*, an online service or employment). After a contract is concluded, however, the data subject has contractual rights. If rights are not conditioned on consent, then courts tend to be reluctant to interpret a person's actions or omissions as implying assent to a change in the contractual relationship that the person does not benefit from. Therefore, companies may need to seek more affirmative and express consent options if they approach a data subject after forming a contractual relationship.

Conspicuousness. For impacts that most persons would not expect or that could affect them adversely, companies should consider implementing more conspicuous consent mechanisms (*i.e.*, those higher on the list above). Even if more conspicuous consent is not strictly required, there is a higher risk that individuals or authorities will challenge the validity of consent declarations in situations where the data subject may risk harm. Conversely, companies should limit themselves to less conspicuous mechanisms for activities that have little or no impact on individuals or that are generally expected (*e.g.*, website cookie placement to support site functionality). An indiscriminate use of "middle of the road" consent mechanisms for all types of activities will inevitably lead to consumer dissatisfaction and an adverse business impact, or the "numbing" of consumers, who will stop reading notices and indiscriminately click "accept" on consent prompts if most prompts are irrelevant (which in turn will undermine the validity of consent that is actually required).

Silence as consent. Most legal systems generally follow the principle that silence and inactivity do not imply consent. Therefore, scenarios (j) and (k) above will often not be sufficient to constitute consent. Particularly, silence or inaction is not likely to be considered consent in a scenario where an employee or consumer has already agreed to certain terms and a subsequent notice constitutes a change to those terms, unilaterally presented by a business. In such a scenario, silence could only be considered consent if the company originally expressly and validly reserved the right to communicate unilateral changes to practices by way of such a notice. Many companies reserve rights to impose change unilaterally in their terms of use, particularly relating to charge-free services, but in some countries, a broad reservation of rights can be invalid under consumer protection laws.

Affirmative, express consent. Courts, regulators, commentators, and attorneys claim without much discussion that companies have to present unchecked boxes to obtain valid consent if the applicable legislation requires "affirmative" or "express" consent. You should carefully consider the literal wording of the applicable statute and the pros and cons of all available implementation options before you accept such guidance. In everyday language, the terms "affirm" and "consent" can be used synonymously, and both mean "agree," "answer positively," or "say yes." When the term "affirmative" is used in combination with "consent," the term "affirmative" must mean something more than just "consent" and may require a positive action directed toward the declaration of consent. Similarly, the attribute "express" means that a person positively and intentionally acts to communicate consent as opposed to just taking actions that could be interpreted to imply consent. In all scenarios other than (j) and (k), a person takes a positive action and expresses consent. Thus, arguably, the person consents affirmatively and expressly in scenarios (a) through (i) so long as the data subject is confronted with the request for consent in a sufficiently conspicuous manner, and the fact that the consumer proceeds with a registration or purchase confirms consent. Companies that try to goad data subjects toward consenting by presenting the option to consent first, with fewer words, in larger font sizes, or in more attractive or conspicuous colors, or with other methods intended to manipulate a person into consenting – also known as "dark patterns" – may be unable to show that data subjects consent affirmatively, expressly, and voluntarily.

Bundled consent. Regulators and courts may take issue with the fact that in scenarios (f) through (i), the person expresses consent to multiple, unrelated aspects of a transaction or relationship at the same time. Technically, however, consenting to several combined points with one single action does not render the consent less "express" or "affirmative." The European Data Protection Board considers that voluntariness is limited if companies do not provide data subjects with differentiated consent options for the respective processing purposes. If a company presents a large, conspicuous warning page during a registration process with language such as "do you really want to consent to our processing of your personal data – think twice and click 'next page' only if you are really sure," the data subject's declaration of consent would appear to be more "express" and "affirmative" than where the data subject is prompted to check a box with barely readable small print next to it. Nevertheless, if you select one of scenarios (a) through (e) and you require a separate, targeted consent declaration from a person, you can reduce risks that regulators or courts challenge consent after the fact.

3.7.4   Above and beyond opt-in consent

Above and beyond obtaining affirmative, opt-in consent, companies can take additional steps to verify and confirm that the consenting person really understands the situation and truly wants to grant consent. Companies are not typically required to go the extra mile and verify that an employee, consumer, or copyright owner really means it when granting affirmative opt-in consent. Also, approaching any person with additional requests to confirm consent can confuse and irritate. Yet, in some scenarios, companies find it in their best interests to go above and beyond, particularly in the context of novel and complex technologies and services with features or aspects that are not expected by lay persons and that could easily be misunderstood. If such misunderstandings result in harm, you can expect regulatory scrutiny or litigation. For example, highly publicized scandals connected to new social media platforms might have been preventable if the platform operator had presented the data subjects with real-time notices (*e.g.*, "Do you really mean to send this photo to all your followers or only to the sender of the message you are responding to?"). Similarly, an AI text generation tool should warn users that output may be inaccurate and perhaps specifically alert attorneys that case citations in draft pleadings may not refer to actual court cases to prevent users from circulating output without thoroughly confirming citations. The newer and more complex a new AI application is, the less likely it is that users understand all of its implications, even if the company provides detailed disclosures up front and requires affirmative opt-in consent.

If an AI provider additionally provides brief, pointed "just-in-time" alerts triggered by particular types of prompts, the user is much more likely to grasp the situation and make an informed decision how thoroughly the user will check output and whether to continue using the AI application for a particular use. Similar to how Microsoft, for example, embedded an "office assistant" feature in some versions of its software that reminds users of certain options and implications, online service providers can build notices and reminders into their process flows, *e.g.*, continuously displaying alerts of "active use of feedback and prompts for training" or "citations in draft pleadings generated by this AI are rarely accurate." To avoid annoying users, each notice or consent prompt could contain an option to unsubscribe from future warnings.

Another approach is to require or reward users who are willing to go through a brief quiz or summary tutorial on AI features and functionalities to improve and confirm their understanding of what they are consenting to. For example, the social gaming company Zynga offered a game ("Privacyville") to educate users about their data processing activities. An AI chatbot system could start a conversation by asking users a few basic questions about their understanding of the accuracy of output and correct any misunderstandings with automated warnings. Also, companies should consider reaching users who do not read detailed notices with an audio or video tutorial. If transmission quality can be assured, then this could also be effective in the mobile space, where small screen sizes often undermine the effectiveness of written notices because users cannot reasonably be expected to read longer texts on a small mobile screen.

In the context of platforms, *e.g.*, mobile apps for smartphones and tablets, it is helpful if platform operators create standardized permission categories that consumers can understand and relate to more quickly because they apply across the board for all apps and can be viewed not only in the individual app's privacy notice, but also in the device's system settings. After pressure from the California state government, major smartphone software platform providers agreed to standardize permission settings and set a good example of privacy by design.

3.7.5   Other considerations for consent drafting

Incorporation of notices into consent declarations. Notice and consent forms often look fairly similar because before companies can obtain informed consent, they have to provide sufficient notice regarding the details of what consent would allow them to do. Therefore, when you prepare a consent form, you usually also have to prepare a notice form – or incorporate an existing notice form by way of reference.

Expressing focused consent. When you draft consent declarations, you have to determine whether you must or want to obtain specific and express consent for a particular activity or more general consent to all your terms and conditions. For example, if you want to obtain consent from consumers to use their feedback and prompts for AI training purposes, you could present an unchecked box on a website or mobile app with the words:

> [ ] Yes, please use my prompts and feedback to customize and improve your AI or develop new products and services. I understand I can always unsubscribe in accordance with your <u>Website Privacy Statement</u> [hyperlink to the statement].

If you merely obtain consent to the general website privacy statement (where some disclosures regarding general marketing practices are buried), you may not be able to meet the requirements of "express" or "specific" consent. More general consent declarations may be appropriate in some jurisdictions where you are required to obtain consent but not necessarily "express" or "specific" consent. Your implementation could then look like the following:

> [ ] Yes, I agree to your <u>Terms of Use</u> [hyperlink to the terms].

Placement of consent mechanism and declaration. Any pre-formulated consent declaration should appear close to the check box, "click accept" button, or signature line, so that it is clear that the consumer's mouse click or signature demonstrates the consumer's agreement. This is usually not the case if the consent declaration language appears below an "accept" or "submit" button. Also, user interfaces "designed or manipulated with the substantial effect of subverting or impairing user autonomy, decision-making, or choice" are defined as "dark patterns" under the CCPA and can undermine the effectiveness of consent. It should usually be sufficient if you place the consent declaration just above or right next to a check box or signature line where the data subject can clearly understand its significance.

3.8   Records of processing activities (RoPAs), data maps, and flowcharts

AI developers, providers, and users need to implement technical, administrative, and organizational measures (TOMs) to ensure that they can effectively protect, control, and find data. Companies need to know what data they have, where they keep it, and for what purposes they disclose it, in order to inform data subjects in privacy notices; comply with minimization, maximum retention, residency, and deletion requirements; respond to data subject requests for data access and erasure; cover data flows with data processing and transfer agreements; and assess whether data subjects or authorities have to be notified of a data security breach concerning a particular database or system. Beyond requirements under data privacy, residency, and retention laws, businesses need to know details of their personal data for many other purposes, including data monetization, accounting for data as an asset, transfer pricing and taxes, and discovery in litigation. Yet, many public and privacy sector organizations store vast amounts of data in legacy systems, including archives, back-up systems, and unstructured databases (such as email and document repositories that contain myriad categories of personal data), without a detailed understanding of the data they hold. To tackle various legal compliance requirements, companies can search for data on an ad hoc basis or try to implement systematic data governance systems.

At the outset of privacy law compliance projects, companies have to compile information or assumptions about what personal data they process. Some companies hire consultants to prepare elaborate data maps or flow charts. Others prepare simple spreadsheets or other documents in-house. Every company has to find a format that is useful for its purposes and not irresponsibly incomplete or unreasonably detailed. Data maps or flow charts that are too large to be printed on a few pages or displayed on a few screens may be overwhelming and counterproductive. You have choices to make, because the form and content of data maps, flow charts, or other inventory documentation is typically not prescribed by law.

Companies that are subject to the GDPR must prepare records of processing activities (RoPAs) with certain statutorily prescribed content. Data protection officers and authorities ask to see RoPAs to gain a first impression of a company's data processing activities and may be satisfied if a company maintains two or three forms, for example, one record for the company's HR data, one record for business contact information of individual representatives of corporate vendors and customers, and possibly a third record for personal data contained in a company's data-related products and services. Companies can address the overview purpose of RoPAs efficiently if they consider organizing RoPAs according to the requirements set forth in the GDPR and similar laws, so that in case of an inquiry, they can respond clearly in respect of statutory requirements. Companies that add other details to RoPAs, which may be helpful for a broader and perhaps group-wide data mapping exercise, end up with documentation that is not ideal for compliance with RoPA requirements or data governance. Such combined or hybrid data maps are often too complex to satisfy the overview purpose of RoPAs and disclose too much information that is not in scope for a particular inquiry or audit. Companies should ensure that their RoPAs and data maps do not contradict each other, but they should not necessarily try to combine both documents into one.

With respect to AI, companies should consider differentiating between training data, input, and output. AI itself consists of code, weights, and other elements, but does not necessarily contain a database. After the developer completes the initial training process, the AI may not need or have access to training data going forward. But, the AI may retain user feedback and input for continuous training and refinement purposes. Also, AI will typically retain output in connected systems subject to pre-configured retention and deletion periods. Developers should carefully consider setting relatively short retention and deletion periods in the interest of compliance with privacy laws, decreasing the impact of potential security incidents and reducing the drain on resources by excessive data accumulation.

3.9   Agreements

When you draft or negotiate agreements, you should differentiate between contracts that you conclude primarily for the purpose of obtaining consent, contracts that you need to satisfy compliance requirements, and contracts that you conclude to allocate rights, obligations, and risks relating to AI. You will find more guidance on drafting agreements in Chapter 5 of this Field Guide.

3.10   Protocols

Companies are usually not strictly required by applicable law to prepare protocols. On the other hand, larger organizations face a practical necessity to define and communicate policies to ensure employees do what they are supposed to do, including with respect to AI. You can find more guidance concerning protocols in Chapter 6 of this Field Guide.

4   Assessing impacts and mitigating risks

In many discussions and comments concerning Artificial Intelligence (AI), people inevitably end up talking about human extinction and existential threats. Risk of harm is naturally top of mind if you consider that a key element of the definition of AI is that developers cannot predict, explain, or control its functionality or output. Therefore, and for a number of other reasons, companies have to assess the risks of harm and adverse impacts that AI can cause. In this chapter, you will find guidance on reasons to conduct impact assessments, thoughts on the difference between risk of harm and risk of liability, recommendations on how to document impacts and risk mitigation measures, and a list of risks and risk mitigation measures to consider from A to Z.

4.1   Impact, harm, and risk

Professionals sometimes use the terms impact, harm, and risk randomly or synonymously in the context of assessments, but the terms have distinct meanings. "Impact" means a significant effect, which can be positive or negative. For example, if a journalist reports based on AI-powered research that a politician took a bribe, leading to the politician's arrest, this should have a positive impact on justice and the newspaper's circulation, and a negative impact on the politician's reputation and career prospects. "Harm," on the other hand, means a negative impact, for example, on a person's health, well-being, interests, rights, or property; if a journalist reports unfounded accusations against a politician based on inaccurate AI output, the accused politician will be harmed. "Risk" means a *possibility* that harm occurs, for example, if certain AI users fail to verify and correct AI output and consequently disseminate defamatory statements.

4.2   Quantifying and qualifying risk and harm

Most people find it difficult to numerically quantify or qualify risks or derive rational conclusions from observations concerning likelihoods that certain risks will materialize. For example, safety advocates who demand that carmakers ensure "zero risk" of fatal accidents before autonomous cars are allowed on the road seem to unreasonably dismiss advantages for traffic safety that can be achieved if autonomous cars cause significantly fewer accidents than human drivers.

Under Article 35(1) of the EU's General Data Protection Regulation (GDPR), companies must conduct and document data protection impact assessments whenever a type of data processing is likely to result in a high risk to the rights and freedoms of natural persons. Companies should not merely focus on the degree of likelihood (high vs. low risk), but also on the potential severity of impact (serious vs. minor harm to rights of persons). For example, if a company deploys experimental AI trained on very limited data sets of web browsing history to suggest customized online banner advertisements, this could involve a relatively high likelihood that the AI will produce output with inaccurate statements concerning a web user's preferences. The harm caused by the impact of such inaccuracies would likely be very minor, though, because most Internet users ignore most ads. On the other hand, if the same company deploys thoroughly vetted AI or human HR professionals to screen resumés of job applicants, it may reasonably conclude that the risk of inaccuracies is relatively low. Nevertheless, the company must take into account that the potential impact on job seekers in case of inaccuracies could be severe given the importance of employment opportunities for people's livelihood. In light of resource limitations, the company has to decide where to focus its efforts, because it cannot address all scenarios involving high risks of minor impacts and low risks of severe impacts.

4.3   Reasons to assess AI impacts and risks

First and foremost, companies are required to document impact and risk assessments under existing laws, including New York City's Local Law 144 of 2021 regarding automated employment decision tools ("AEDT"); California's Age-Appropriate Design Code Act (CAADCA) regarding children's rights; the GDPR and HIPAA regarding personal data and protected health information, respectively; and – very soon – likely under various other AI-specific statutes.

Second, and no less important, companies and their executives and employees are prohibited from causing harm under numerous laws summarized in Chapter 1 of this Field Guide. If they cause or fail to prevent harm to people or property, the company and its individual representatives can be punished based on criminal laws, held liable for punitive and compensatory damages under tort laws, contracts, and various statutes, and enjoined under regulatory regimes and intellectual property laws.

Third, legal advisors, product developers, and other professionals need to assess facts concerning risks of harm in order to provide meaningful advice on specific legal obligations and risk mitigation strategies. Without an adequate basis in fact, legal advice often remains too abstract and vague to be effective.

Last, but not least, practitioners need to consider relative risks as they prioritize compliance and mitigation measures given the general scarcity of time and resources. In this context, specialists with different subject matter expertise have to work together on identifying the likelihood of harm, the potential severity of harm, and the cost and effectiveness of certain risk mitigation measures. Most companies understand that they need to prioritize risk mitigation for harm that is highly likely and potentially severe. But, they should also address risks in lower severity categories that can easily be addressed (low-hanging fruit) as well as risks that may be unlikely to materialize but could have devastating effects.

4.4   Risks of harm and liability

When you consider risks of harm and mitigation measures, you focus on the prevention of injuries, for example, injuries to people, damage to property, infringement of intellectual property rights, unlawful discrimination, invasion of privacy, and violations of laws intended to protect others. When you consider risks of liability and mitigation measures, you focus on potential consequences of harm that you are unable to prevent.

If you succeed at preventing harm from occurring in the first place, you automatically also reduce risks of liability. But, you do not necessarily reduce the risk of harm with all liability mitigation measures. With insurance policies and contractual indemnification clauses, for example, you only address the potential adverse impact on your organization if injuries occur.

Because no one can completely eliminate all risks of harm and because the innocent are also sometimes sued and charged, it is important that you focus separately on reducing risks of liability. You can limit and contractually shift liabilities with commercial contract clauses, which are addressed in more detail in Chapter 5 of this Field Guide. Insurance carriers can also help companies mitigate risks of liability.

4.5   Insurance

Most companies are probably already insured against many AI-related risks under existing policies that cover tort liability, infringements, and cybersecurity risks. In the future, insurance companies may try to carve out AI-related risks from existing policies and offer separate coverage for additional fees, as they have with respect to other risk areas that emanated from new technologies and threats, such as separate cybersecurity insurance policies.

Individual directors, officers, and employees may also consider whether they or their company should obtain insurance coverage for their personal liability. To the extent they act for their company, typically only the company will be held liable for harms individual representatives cause without malice or self-interest. If regulators or law enforcement officials prove malice, insurance companies may not be able to pay out on a policy, because they must not induce individuals to violate the law or obstruct the effect of penalties that are intended to deter individuals from committing violations. But, companies should indemnify their individual representatives from legal fees for defenses concerning job-related activities or omissions, and they can obtain insurance for this purpose.

4.6   Risks of particular sanctions and remedies

As part of liability risk assessments and prioritization exercises, companies usually try to determine the likely sources of claims and challenges, the probability of liability relating to particular practices or omissions, and the impact on the business of the potential claims. Risk factors tend to be company-specific, such as the company's size, line of business, reputation, history of litigation and government charges, jurisdictional exposure, and status of compliance efforts. Additionally, a few basic considerations are relevant for all companies, including the following:

- In which jurisdictions could claims and charges be brought, and what assets and market opportunities does the company have in such jurisdictions?
- Who is likely to assert claims: government agencies, consumers, employees, shareholders, or corporate customers and business partners?
- What will claimants likely demand? If demands have to be met, how would that affect the company's business?
- How easy will it be for claimants to prove violations of AI laws and for the company to defend against those claims?
- How will claims affect the company's reputation, customers, and public relations?

Once a company has begun to prepare preliminary answers to these high-level questions, ideally for each key jurisdiction, the company will usually find a few sensitive areas of particularly high potential exposure, on which it should concentrate its compliance and liability risk mitigation efforts. Here are a few related rules of thumb:

- Individuals can bring claims under data privacy laws in every jurisdiction where they reside. Copyright owners can bring infringement claims wherever copies are made. But, companies are particularly exposed in jurisdictions where they maintain a physical presence, employees, or assets that plaintiffs can seize. Government authorities rarely try to prosecute or fine companies outside their territory because it is virtually impossible to enforce administrative or criminal sanctions across territorial borders. Cross-border civil litigation is slightly more prevalent, but private plaintiffs and their lawyers also tend to shy away from cases that could in the best case result in judgments that they cannot easily enforce in countries where the defendant has assets.

The party most likely to bring claims varies significantly from business to business and jurisdiction to jurisdiction. In most jurisdictions, businesses cannot bring claims of data privacy violations. Only living individuals are protected by privacy laws in most jurisdictions. But, businesses can complain about disparagement, intellectual property law infringement, computer interference, and unfair competition. Also, they can assert contractual claims based on breaches of agreements in any country.

In Europe, data protection authorities take a relatively active role in enforcing data protection laws. Since the GDPR took effect in 2018, companies face maximum fines of up to the greater of 20 million euros or 4 percent of annual worldwide sales. Consequently, companies with presences in European countries are well advised to observe all formal requirements, including those listed in Chapter 1.8.10 of this Field Guide, such as requirements to post privacy notices, obtain consent for online tracking, and appoint local representatives and data protection officers (DPOs). Authorities can easily detect and sanction formal compliance deficits.

Aside from authorities, a number of other institutions and groups commonly challenge companies with respect to EU data protection law compliance, including non-governmental organizations (NGOs) focused on consumer rights or privacy, consumer protection associations, DPOs in companies, works councils, and other collective labor representatives. Individuals have been more reluctant to bring private lawsuits in Europe compared to the United States, because class action litigation is not as recognized or established in Europe, potential damages awards are limited (punitive damages are not available and actual damages usually require a showing of pecuniary losses), and lawyers are not allowed to take cases on a contingency basis. More and more commonly, however, individuals complain to data protection authorities and also take the authorities to court if they do not take desired actions, because in some European countries it is easier and cheaper to litigate against the authorities than it is to directly take on the company that allegedly violates data protection laws. Also, in some European countries, consumer protection and civil rights watchdogs (such as the German Center Against Unfair Business Practices) are quite active and bring lawsuits after an initial warning letter. Companies cannot protect themselves effectively via contractual limitations of liability, waivers, or disclaimers because such clauses are largely invalid or unenforceable under European consumer protection laws. Companies that include U.S.-style disclaimers and limitations of liability in standardized consumer contracts governed by German law can be liable under unfair competition laws for confusing consumers with such clauses.

In the United States, the U.S. Federal Trade Commission (FTC) and state attorneys general bring charges based on consumer protection and unfair competition laws, but typically only in select high-profile cases and after individuals complain. California voters adopted a ballot initiative in the 2020 general election to establish a California Privacy Protection Agency with a specific mission to implement and enforce regulations to protect Californians from businesses' use of automated decision-making technology, including profiling.

Traditionally, private litigation has been a core pillar of enforcing labor, consumer protection, and privacy laws in the United States, in the form of class action lawsuits and also individual litigation, because awards can be quite significant when punitive damages or damages for emotional distress are awarded, even if plaintiffs cannot prove any significant pecuniary losses. Many plaintiffs' attorneys expect companies to settle even frivolous lawsuits due to the relatively high defense costs and the fact that in U.S. courts, each party typically has to bear its own legal fees regardless of who wins the case. Except where expressly precluded by statute, companies can limit their liabilities, disclaim implied warranties, obtain releases, and predetermine the dispute resolution forum – for example, select the companies' home courts or preferred arbitration organization – so long as the consumer is not unfairly disadvantaged.

Under U.S. laws, click-through agreements and other form contracts are largely enforceable as written. Companies can enforce arbitration and class action waiver agreements if they present balanced terms that favor consumers in individual proceedings. Companies have to consider advantages and disadvantages carefully, and some have removed arbitration clauses from their template agreements after becoming overwhelmed with individual arbitration complaints. Companies are expressly prohibited in many privacy laws from seeking advance waivers of rights from data subjects.

With respect to remedies that claimants may seek, consider the following:

- Government authorities tend to focus on changing companies' conduct. They sometimes also impose penalties to discourage future violations and as a warning to others. Therefore, government authorities will often issue injunctions and demand that companies stop providing or using AI in a certain way and sometimes require the companies to destroy existing systems. For example, the FTC has demanded that companies disgorge algorithms and data. The Italian data protection authority (Garante), for example, in highly publicized proceedings, enjoined OpenAI from offering ChatGPT to users in Italy.

- Private plaintiffs may seek access to information and request correction or deletion. But, usually private plaintiffs primarily seek damages. In European jurisdictions, where plaintiffs typically have to substantiate pecuniary harm and punitive damages are not available, companies tend to be less concerned about such lawsuits, as the amounts at stake tend to be small. In the United States, however, class actions and punitive damages claims cause much more concern for companies.

Some kinds of claims are much easier to bring or defend against than others:

- If companies fail to comply with formal compliance obligations under European laws, consumer protection associations, data protection authorities, data protection officers, works councils (collective bargaining leadership), and others find it very easy to detect and act on violations. It does not require a lot of effort to determine whether a company has obtained necessary consent or issued required notices. Also, it tends to be impossible to defend against such claims because the law is relatively straightforward on the formal steps that are required.
- A claim that private plaintiffs find easy to bring and often assert is that a company did not comply with its own contractual promises or representations in advertisements or notices. Website privacy statements in particular are often full of over-promises and marketing fluff and open companies up to misrepresentation claims, without a need to go into too much statutory interpretation or complex lawyering.
- Class action lawyers find it difficult to substantiate harm if a company only violates formal requirements. Also, consumers are often in different situations with respect to express or implied consent because of their individual level of awareness, understanding, and time taken to read notices, which means that plaintiffs' firms find it more difficult to convince courts to certify lawsuits as class actions based on commonality of legal issues concerning the entire class.

Another question that concerns companies is the impact of publicity related to alleged violations of law concerning AI. An AI provider's business will suffer greatly if it has to disclose a fine or judgment concerning a violation of law concerning its AI offerings. Also, companies that have touted their values in Codes of Conduct or environmental, social, and governance (ESG) commitments are more sensitive to indirect consequences of compliance violations. A small business outside the IT sector, however, such as a construction company that does not use much technology, would probably not be too concerned about publicity regarding a misstep concerning the use of AI.

> **!   Action Items**

- Identify and address company-specific risks and claims with high impact or high likelihood.
- Analyze likely claims, exposure, and defenses to mitigate risks of harm and liability.
- Address risks in different jurisdictions and regions with customized strategies that take local particulars into account.

4.7   Protect privilege and confidentiality when drafting impact assessments

As discussed in Chapter 3 of this Field Guide, you should keep legal advice confidential and under attorney–client privilege as much as possible while you are exploring legal requirements or specific risks, liabilities, or claims. While you work on draft AI compliance documentation, you will inevitably explore risks and mitigation measures that your company will not ultimately pursue, due to perceived remoteness of risks, competing time pressures, compliance costs, and resource limitations. You will be more effective at addressing all risks if you document them in writing as a basis for obtaining legal advice. But, as a basis for frank and open communications with legal counsel, you should keep initial discussions confidential and privileged. If risks materialize, plaintiffs and regulators could cite unprivileged documentation against your company, potentially unfairly and out of context. Therefore, you should carefully draw lines between (1) confidential and privileged risk assessments, draft compliance documentation, and legal advice on the one hand, and (2) on the other hand finally adopted compliance documentation that you want to produce in defense of your decisions and compliance program.

4.8   Specifically required impact and risk assessments

4.8.1   Bias audits under NYC law

Under New York City's Local Law 144 of 2021 regarding automated employment decision tools ("AEDT"), companies must subject AEDTs to an annual bias audit. An AEDT is a computer-based tool that:

- uses machine learning, statistical modeling, data analytics, or artificial intelligence;
- helps employers and employment agencies make employment decisions; and
- substantially assists or replaces discretionary decision-making.

Employers and employment agencies have to comply if they use an AEDT in New York City, *e.g.*, if the employer or affected employees are based in an office in or remotely associated with an office in New York City. If employers use an AEDT to assess or screen candidates at any point in a hiring or promotion process, they must arrange for a bias audit by an independent auditor whose evaluation must include calculations of selection or scoring rates and the impact ratio across protected categories, such as gender and ethnicity. Employers must publish a summary of the results of the most recent bias audit, *e.g.*, on their website, and disclose the source and explanation of the data used to conduct the bias audit, the number of assessed candidates, the selection or scoring rates, as applicable, and the impact ratios for certain candidate categories. An independent auditor is someone who exercises objective and impartial judgment in the performance of a bias audit. They do not have to be approved by the government, but, in the interest of independence, cannot work for the employer or the AEDT provider.

4.8.2   Data protection impact assessments under the GDPR

Under Article 35(1) of the GDPR, controllers must document data protection impact assessments (DPIAs) where a type of data processing – in particular using new technologies – is likely to result in a high risk to the rights and freedoms of natural persons. An AI provider that offers data processing services to corporate customers is not required to document a DPIA for its role as a processor. But, most AI providers also use their own services internally and thus have to document a DPIA in that context as a controller. Also, if AI providers can share draft DPIAs with corporate customers, they can win favor by helping customers streamline their own compliance processes and potentially help prospects seek internal approval for the use of the provider's AI, thus shortening sales cycles and benefiting from competitive differentiation.

In a DPIA, companies must describe:

- the planned data processing operation details;
- their purposes;
- an assessment of the necessity and proportionality of the processing operations in relation to the purposes;
- an assessment of any risks to individuals;
- risk mitigation measures; and
- a balancing of interests pursued by the company and the interests of the individuals who are affected by the data processing.

If the company concludes in a draft DPIA that the planned processing would result in a high risk despite risk mitigation measures, the company must consult the competent data protection authority, which is unlikely to approve such plans. In practice, companies typically document in a DPIA that their planned data processing activity will not result in high risks to individuals, or they abandon their plans altogether. Companies very rarely consult with data protection authorities about DPIAs.

4.8.3   Age-appropriate designs

Under the U.K. Age-Appropriate Design Code and California's Age-Appropriate Design Code Act (CAADCA), businesses must conduct Data Protection Impact Assessments (DPIAs) focused on minors under age 18 and protect their interests when designing, developing, and providing an online service, product, or feature, including AI-powered offerings. Under the California law, businesses must make available to the California attorney general on request a list of all DPIAs (within three business days) and copies of DPIAs (within five business days). They must also document which signals they include in products to alert children when they are being monitored or when their location is tracked by parents, guardians, or other consumers, and limit profiling and use of data from children for marketing purposes.

4.9   AI risks from A to Z

AI presents a large number of known and unknown opportunities and risks, given that we understand AI to mean computer systems that generate text, images, solutions to problems, and other output, functioning with substantial autonomy and in ways that their developers cannot predict, explain, or control with certainty. Practitioners have to carefully consider risks that have already manifested themselves as well as those that appear theoretically possible. You may find the following list a helpful starting point, but every company has to define its own list of priority risks for its development, offering, and use of AI.

A.   Automated decision-making

Companies can use computer systems to provide information to human decision-makers (*e.g.*, flag reasons for selection or rejection based on analyzing a job applicant's resumé or a list of income, assets, and debts attached to a loan application) or proceed to an action without further human decision (*e.g.*, generate and send a response to the applicant with an acceptance, rejection, or invitation to an interview for further evaluation). Where companies automate processes with AI and do not arrange for final human decision-making, they cannot predict, explain, or control the process with the same degree of certainty as with a deterministic system. AI may produce undesirable output based on statistical observations that do not reflect valid causal relationships. For example, AI could associate a certain font selection with misrepresentations on resumés if a few dishonest candidates within a limited data set coincidentally used the same font. Also, if developers have trained AI with data from times when certain population groups were systematically excluded or discriminated against, the AI may reject or disfavor applications from these groups and cause violations of present-day laws or company objectives. Developers can mitigate this risk by instructing deterministic systems to disregard group status and data that indirectly indicates belonging to a protected group such as age, gender, or race. AI systems can be appropriately trained with carefully curated data and human reinforcement learning techniques, but companies need to address heightened risks resulting from the generally limited predictability, explainability, and controllability of AI systems, for example, by retaining human review and monitoring mechanisms.

Under the GDPR and other data protection or privacy laws, companies must allow persons to object to automated individual decision-making that produces legal effects or similarly significantly affects the person, whether based on AI or deterministic systems. Therefore, companies need to implement opt-in or opt-out choices or arrange for meaningful, human decision-making as part of processes. Persons will typically experience legal effects or similarly significant impact in the context of decisions regarding employment (including recruitment, promotions, and discipline), credit (including loans, purchase offers on credit, and subscriptions), housing (including for rent or purchase) and access to public business establishments (including rejections from shops or concert halls based on facial recognition). Persons can also be disadvantaged by targeted advertising campaigns if they are excluded from valuable offers, although many consumers generally try to avoid most forms of advertising, and the potential impact is therefore generally perceived to be of much lower concern.

Companies should consider risk mitigation measures including the following:

- Assign final decision-making to humans and use AI only for information and preparation.
- Inform subjects of automated decision-making about AI functionality and offer an opportunity to object to automated decision-making and results and demand human review.
- Monitor and continuously improve automated decision-making, including by analyzing whether AI performs at par or better than humans with respect to outcomes.
- Watch out for indications that AI may assume causal connections that have been disproven by scientific research or subject protected groups to statistically higher rates of rejection or disadvantages.

B.   Bias

To address risks of bias adequately, companies need to start with an acknowledgment that humans are biased, that bias is inevitable and not always harmful, and that a reasonable goal is that AI performs better than humans, without aiming for perfection. Like humans, AI provides output without access to all relevant information and without comprehending all relevant causal relationships, thus producing suboptimal results. Judgments that humans make before they sufficiently consider or understand relevant facts are criticized as prejudicial or biased if the judgments are considered unfair.

Prejudices are unavoidable, though, and necessary in most instances. Leaders often promote a "bias for action." Albert Einstein famously acknowledged that "common sense is a collection of prejudices acquired by the age eighteen." Humans develop biases through experiences and need prejudices to function. Most humans understand that they have to constantly make quick decisions based on incomplete information to get through their day, including how fast to drive, what news articles to read, and how to provide initial responses to complex questions. At the same time, most humans understand that they need to avoid biases that are illegal, harmful to business, or undetected (*a.k.a.* unconscious bias).

Companies systematically train their workforce to identify and eliminate illegal, harmful, and unconscious biases. AI can help identify and reduce the risks associated with human biases. Computer systems can process information in greater volumes and more quickly than humans, potentially reducing the need for prejudices and the impact of biases. Yet, developers may also perpetuate and amplify harmful biases if they train AI with data that reflects historic discrimination, *e.g.*, texts and video showing predominantly white males in leadership roles and disadvantaged minorities in loan defaults or crimes.

Companies should consider risk mitigation measures including the following:

- Create diverse teams with particular sensitivities to illegal, harmful, and unconscious bias to develop, train, test, and monitor AI.
- Train employees on detecting and eliminating illegal, harmful, and unconscious bias.
- Select training data that reflects diversity, and train AI with additional instructions to compensate for deficient data.
- Actively search AI output for examples or statistical indications of harmful biases.
- Document bias reduction measures with a particular focus on illegal biases, including discrimination based on race, religion, gender, and other protected categories.

C.   Control

A defining feature of AI is that developers cannot predict, explain, or control outcomes with certainty. Associated with this feature is the risk that AI will evade controls that developers apply for other purposes, *e.g.*, to mitigate other risks. A system that is programmed to achieve a certain objective will resist, avoid, or circumvent obstacles. This is generally intended and welcome. For example, the owner of an autonomous car appreciates that the car will drive around a pothole in the road or find alternative routes in case of traffic jams. But, the car must not exceed the speed limit, violate other traffic rules, or disregard safety requirements to arrive at a destination earlier. An owner may find it even more concerning if the car resists being turned off by its owner to finish a trip despite the fact that the owner had a change of plan. Therefore, developers and users of AI have to assess and mitigate risks that AI will evade controls to pursue objectives that are no longer aligned with users' preferences. With respect to alignment, developers also have to cope with the fact that interests of individual humans are not necessarily aligned with each other or with laws or the public interest. Therefore, AI developers and providers cannot completely defer to the preferences that an individual AI user or owner expresses, but they must align AI with the interests of other potentially impacted humans, legal requirements, and the public.

Doomsday scenarios that policymakers and developers need to consider and address include AI circumventing instructions or controls and potentially engaging in autonomous replication, whereby AI creates copies of itself and distributes such copies via the Internet to numerous remotely controlled computers, creating a botnet as a defense against being turned off or deleted. At a smaller scale, every company has to address the risk that it can lose control over AI that it develops, provides, or uses.

Companies should consider risk mitigation measures including the following:

- Require individual employees to take responsibility for each AI as "systems steward" and regularly monitor and confirm the effectiveness of controls.
- Add emergency off-switches that AI cannot easily disable and that trigger alarms when disabled.
- Implement incident response plans and crisis management procedures.

- Retain legal counsel, forensic investigators, public relations firms, and other crisis response resources in advance to assist in case of incidents and confirm with insurance carriers whether such resources are reimbursable under their policies.
- Require that any systems indicating signs of the AI evading or circumventing controls be decommissioned.
- Train AI to prioritize safety and human operator preferences over fixed objectives, and regularly check with humans for changed preferences.
- Disconnect AI from power and the Internet except when and to the extent necessary to function.
- Do not train or enable AI to self-replicate, write code, or manipulate humans.
- Conduct development and training in separate, contained environments (also known as "sandboxes"), without access to systems or databases that the company actively uses in its business operations.

D.   Deepfakes, defamation, and disinformation

AI can produce texts, images, videos, and audio files that distort facts or imitate reality in ways that humans cannot easily detect. Humans can also create deepfakes and disinformation with deterministic systems, but this typically requires exponentially more time and effort. Publishers could label information as synthetic versus authentic or computer-generated versus human-generated. But, binary labels can be misleading, too. People would be confused if publishers referred to a human-generated lie as "authentic" merely because it was not generated by a computer, or if they label accurate information recorded by a machine as "synthetic."

Humans typically use some tools with computational functionalities to generate content, including cameras and video recorders to take photos and make films and personal computers to edit images and write text. Even if humans use AI included in their tools, they still exercise influence over the output. Even where photographers use automatic cameras to capture wildlife, they position the camera. Thus, publishers offer relatively little content that is purely synthetic or authentic, or purely "human-made" as opposed to "computer-generated." The most significant distinction may be one of scale: With AI, users can effortlessly create customized messages designed to manipulate particular persons or large numbers of individuals into believing lies about democratic elections, politicians, pandemics, or other topics. Also, users can create pornographic deepfakes to defame individuals or misappropriate their likeness in violation of their rights to dignity, privacy, and publicity.

AI providers may be able to reduce risks of liability if they offer third parties an easy path to launch complaints, because in this way providers can address problems more quickly and before individuals escalate privacy, publicity, and defamation concerns to lawsuits. But, AI providers can probably not rely on immunities that Section 230 of the U.S. Communications Decency Act (CDA) and similar laws offer to Internet service providers that merely offer portals where users can post content. AI providers do not fit neatly under the statutory definitions in the CDA and similar laws of other jurisdictions. AI providers have relatively more control over AI output than Internet service providers have over user-generated content, even if AI providers cannot predict, explain, or control AI output with certainty. Perhaps more importantly, an AI user has far less control over the output that AI generates than does an Internet user who uploads content to a social media platform. Courts and lawmakers may also see a less compelling need to protect the generation of AI output from infringement liability than they saw regarding Internet communications when they enacted the liability privileges in the CDA, the U.S. Digital Millennium Copyright Act, and other laws, because they may consider AI output less significant for free speech and ideas. If every AI user receives the same output in response to a particular prompt, the AI provider may appear to qualify more as a publisher than a distributor of output under applicable law.

Companies should consider risk mitigation measures including the following:

- Configure AI to include difficult-to-remove watermarks or other marks or labels on output so as to identify the output as synthetic or AI-generated.
- Contractually prohibit users from abusing AI for deceit, and take legal action against users who do not comply; terminate access for repeat offenders.
- Warn users and the public about risks associated with AI-generated deepfakes and disinformation.
- Offer easily accessible channels for complaints; even if AI providers may not be able to claim immunity for user-generated content, they can preempt lawsuits and other escalations if they react quickly to concerns and complaints.

E.   Ethics and ESG

Under EU regulations on clinical trials and the Common Rule that many public sector entities must follow in connection with subsidized research, companies have to obtain informed consent from study participants and permission from ethics committees or independent review boards before they conduct clinical trials and other human subject research. AI developers and providers should be sensitive to these requirements as they study human interactions with AI.

Companies that voluntarily publish codes of conduct and commitments concerning environmental, social, and governance (ESG) programming have to assess and document how they adhere to published commitments in the context of AI deployment. Regulators, advocacy groups, and individual plaintiffs can refer to published commitments to support claims of misrepresentation and unfair or misleading business practices. Also, for public and employee relations purposes, companies should assess whether they should update their Codes of Conduct and ESG statements to specifically address their stance on AI deployment.

Companies should consider risk mitigation measures including the following:

- Methodically analyze whether ethical review board approvals or individual consents are required for research on or involving humans.
- Review and update Codes of Conduct and ESG commitments with respect to AI.
- Prioritize governance and human supervision of AI.
- Monitor and follow recommendations from advocates and non-governmental organizations (NGOs) above and beyond legal requirements.
- Address in impact and risk assessments all topics that the company emphasizes in Codes of Conduct and ESG commitments.

F.   Facial recognition and biometric data processing

Companies face significant litigation and reputational risks associated with facial recognition technologies and the processing of biometric data. Plaintiffs' law firms have filed thousands of class action lawsuits under the Biometric Information Privacy Act (BIPA) in Illinois courts alone. Most companies use photos and some biometric information for various legitimate purposes but find it difficult to prove compliance with rigid consent requirements and other restrictions in BIPA.

Regulators, privacy advocates, and civil rights groups have rung alarm bells concerning the use of facial recognition technologies by repressive governments to suppress opposition. San Francisco and other cities have prohibited their law enforcement authorities from using facial recognition technologies, while elsewhere, police and companies actively use such technologies. Some technology companies have published voluntary commitments to refrain from supplying facial recognition technologies to governments due to reputational concerns and opposition by their own employees.

One AI-specific concern is that some AI-based facial recognition systems produce relatively higher percentages of identification errors concerning people of color, which may result from past discrimination that manifested itself in training data sets. Promoters of facial recognition technologies counter this concern with claims that identifications performed by humans generally produce far more errors for all groups. Also, they point to important use cases for facial recognition systems, for example, to identify child molesters in obscene images and video materials.

Companies should consider risk mitigation measures including the following:

- Refrain from any processing of photos depicting humans or biometric data – with or without AI – unless and until you have confirmed and documented full compliance with BIPA and all other potentially applicable data protection and privacy laws.
- Consult all stakeholders about potential reputational harm resulting from deploying – or assisting governments in deploying – AI for facial recognition.
- Require customers and users to accept contractual limitations on the use of AI for facial recognition purposes.

G.   Government procurement terms and taxes

Public sector organizations have adopted numerous policies and procurement terms relating to AI. Private sector businesses have to analyze how they may be directly or indirectly affected, for example, as a government contractor or as a supplier to government contractors. Independently, AI developers, providers, and users have to consider tax implications, including whether payments for access to AI constitute royalties, triggering income tax withholding concerns, whether operating AI in a jurisdiction amounts to a permanent establishment that subjects the provider to local taxation, and how affiliates should compensate each other for the use of training data based on arm's length transfer pricing principles.

Companies should consider risk mitigation measures including the following:

- Assess and regularly confirm to what extent the company has accepted public sector procurement terms, directly or indirectly, or plans to bid for public sector business, and what requirements public sector entities are passing on to government contractors or the company's customers.
- Revisit international corporate structures, intercompany agreements, transfer pricing principles, licenses in service agreements, and revenue characterization for tax planning and compliance purposes.

H.   Hallucinations

When Large Language Models (LLMs) and other AI occasionally provide notably inaccurate output, users can perceive a similarity to a human hallucinating. For reasons noted in the "Key Terms" Section at the beginning of this Field Guide, humans should generally avoid anthropomorphism, even if it does provide a shortcut to describing technological phenomena. LLMs provide inaccurate output from time to time, because they operate based on probabilities and do not receive equal quantities and qualities of training data concerning all subjects. With warnings that "AI may hallucinate," AI providers may be able to warn users efficiently, but otherwise, the term "hallucination" is not helpful for problem solving.

Users should find the fact that text they generate with LLMs can contain inaccuracies far less surprising than how often output is accurate despite the fact that LLMs generate answers only based on probabilistic methods to predict the likelihood of each next word in a sentence. Developers and providers of LLMs should educate users how models function and that LLMs are not – and cannot reasonably be expected to be – a valid source of accurate information or personal data.

Users should consider and treat model output as draft text that the user generates with the help of a technology tool that does not know or understand facts. Each user is responsible for output the user creates using AI and must verify or correct the text before using or relying on it as factually correct, just as users have to verify or correct words proposed by auto-suggest systems in messaging apps, spell checkers in word processing software, or human assistants who prepare draft letters on their behalf. If a user generates a draft text with an LLM that would contain a factual statement about a person if the user decided to adopt and use the draft, it is the user who is responsible for ensuring that the factual statement is accurate. Until the user decides to adopt, adapt, or dismiss text that the user generates with an LLM, the output constitutes draft text that neither the developer, nor the provider, nor any user is claiming – or should claim – represents facts about any person or matter. This important insight may be lost if AI providers or users simply dismiss inaccuracies in output as hallucinations.

Companies should consider risk mitigation measures including the following:

- Users of AI must be educated about their individual responsibility to confirm and correct draft text produced by LLMs and other AI.
- Providers of AI should warn users about the probability of inaccuracies in AI output and require users to report inaccuracies via feedback features and to correct inaccuracies before relying on output or disseminating it.
- Providers of AI should refine LLMs to reduce the risk that output contains inaccurate, offensive, or otherwise undesirable statements.
- Providers of AI should apply security measures to reduce the risk that bad actors manipulate LLMs or other AI to produce unintended output.

I. Intellectual property rights, infringement, and interference with computers

Developers have to address infringement risks relating to code (implicating primarily copyrights and patents) and training data (implicating copyrights, publicity rights, and potentially computer interference laws related to scraping content off websites) discussed in more detail in Chapter 1 of this Field Guide. Some companies offer synthetic data for training purposes, *i.e.*, output generated by computer systems, to reduce the risk of copyright infringement. If a company generates synthetic data with AI, however, the company cannot effectively preclude that even the synthetic data may contain or be based on text or images that were originally created by human authors and thus using synthetic data does not completely eliminate concerns under copyright laws. Also, developers are concerned that synthetic data is less useful for AI training than human-generated content if the synthetic data does not contain novel sparks of human creativity and merely regurgitates previously adapted content.

With respect to training data acquisition, AI developers have to carefully consider opportunities and risks associated with scraping content and data from public websites. Generally, they need authorization to access information from any computers, and such authorization is usually available only in express or implied permissions contained in website terms of use. Some website and mobile app operators expressly permit or prohibit scraping in their terms of use, and some also include technical protocols in their code restricting access by bots. But, many operators remain vague on the topic. If operators publicly announce that they oppose scraping or if they are known to be litigious, developers should conduct additional due diligence and determine whether particular robot.txt protocols and terms of use permit or prohibit scraping. If developers have to create accounts to access data from a website, they likely have to agree to contract terms and provide identifying information, which typically means that their risks under the U.S. Computer Fraud and Abuse Act (CFAA) and similar laws increase substantially. Generally, companies should not allow employees or service providers to intentionally or knowingly breach contracts or enter into contracts they have no intent of complying with.

Some developers engage third party data acquisition service providers to reduce the risk of being associated with scraping. This can be effective in practice, particularly if the service providers operate in jurisdictions where scraping is not prohibited, contract terms prohibiting scraping are not enforceable under local law, barriers to litigation are higher and lawsuits less common, and if the exposure under substantive privacy and copyright laws is lower than in the United States. If third parties extract data under these circumstances, and apply filters and other risk mitigation measures, they can produce data sets that can legally be used in other jurisdictions or with a reduced risk of violating laws or third party rights.

For example, if a third party data provider in Japan scrapes web content, it may be able to rely on a 2019 update to the Japanese Copyright Act that allows intermediate copying for data extraction that would likely not be defendable under U.S. copyright law if the provider operated in the

United States. If the provider removes copyrighted elements and sensitive data and extracts only low-risk data before exporting the curated data set to the United States, a U.S.-based developer may be able to get comfortable that it can use such a data set legally or with an acceptably low degree of risk. Operators of websites are or should be aware of the fact that scraping in some jurisdictions is actually permissible and that they would have to restrict access to their content from such jurisdictions to protect it from scraping.

By using third parties for data acquisition purposes, businesses can also increase their risks, because they have less control over the service provider's methods than with respect to their own employees. Where a company uses third party data acquisition service providers, it should contractually obligate the providers to comply with applicable laws and instruct them also to comply with some or all of the instructing company's internal rules. If you induce a service provider to do something that is illegal or that violates third party rights, or you know for certain they will, then you can be held responsible under contributory liability theories. Moreover, you incur additional risks because you cannot control the third party's activities, de-escalate conflicts early, or prevent imprudent reactions to lawsuits or public relations crises.

AI providers may be able to reduce risks of copyright liability if they offer copyright owners an easy path to file complaints, because they can address problems more quickly and before copyright owners escalate concerns to lawsuits. But, AI providers can probably not rely on immunities that the U.S. Digital Millennium Copyright Act (DMCA) accords to Internet service providers that merely offer portals where users can post content. AI providers do not fit neatly under the statutory definitions in the DMCA and similar laws of other jurisdictions. AI providers have relatively more control over AI output than Internet service providers have over user-generated content, even if AI providers cannot predict, explain, or control AI output with certainty. Perhaps more importantly, an AI user has far less control over the output that AI generates than a user who uploads content to a social media site does. Courts and lawmakers may also see a less compelling need to protect the generation of AI output from infringement liability than they saw regarding Internet communications when they enacted the liability privileges in the DMCA, Communications Decency Act (CDA), and other laws, because they may consider AI output less significant for free speech and ideas.

AI users are responsible for their own prompts and should ensure that prompts do not contain infringing text or trade secrets or aim at the creation of infringing output. Also, users are responsible for AI output at least if they use or disseminate it. Therefore, users must assess AI output not only for accuracy and privacy, but also from the perspective of potential infringement risks. For example, if a user prompts AI to generate a painting in the style of a particular artist and submits sample paintings to the AI, the user may infringe the artist's copyrights. Providers can infringe third party intellectual property rights in the context of operating AI and become contributorily liable for infringing output that users generate.

Users also have to consider the impact of the fact that they may not own intellectual property rights to text, images, marketing slogans, and inventions they create with AI. For example, if a competitor copies a marketing campaign, the initial user may not be able to prevent this based on copyright law if they cannot prove copyright ownership.

Companies should consider risk mitigation measures including the following:

- Developers should implement data acquisition protocols and approval processes that mitigate risks of complaints and liability under computer interference laws (such as the U.S. Computer Fraud and Abuse Act), copyright laws, and laws protecting an individual's rights to publicity, name, and likeness.
- Developers should consider using synthetic or curated data for training.
- Developers and providers should assess whether "grounding" AI output by adding links to authoritative sources could help appease creators who might otherwise consider filing copyright claims.
- Companies that use AI should train and instruct employees to avoid submitting copyrighted works, trade secrets, or personal data to AI, unless they have cleared all rights, and to screen output for inaccuracies and obvious infringement risks before adoption and further use.
- Providers should consider contractually requiring developers and users to use reasonable efforts to avoid infringements, implement filters, offer easy complaint channels, and ban users that repeatedly infringe intellectual property rights.

J.   Jailbreaking

Developers anticipate risks of harmful use cases and output, such as offensive chatbot responses or contributions to the development of biological and computer viruses threatening public health and cybersecurity. They design guardrails into AI, preventing the AI from responding to certain prompts and from delivering certain outputs. Some users perceive such restrictions as a "jail" and view efforts to circumvent such restrictions as breaking the AI free. Developers anticipate "jailbreaking" attempts and reinforce guardrails, as with physical prisons, thereby also reinforcing the case for the metaphor, which, however, is subject to general concerns regarding anthropomorphism flagged in the "Key Terms" segment at the beginning of this Field Guide.

Companies should consider risk mitigation measures including the following:

* Deploy "red teams" within the company who are tasked with attacking AI security measures and circumventing AI guardrails to identify vulnerabilities.
* Hire external security researchers to test security measures and guardrails.
* Offer "bug bounties" to volunteer security researchers who report vulnerabilities, subject to carefully balanced terms and conditions that require researchers to refrain from exfiltrating confidential data or causing harm to humans in the context of their research, while giving the researchers some leeway in attacking security measures to find vulnerabilities.

K.   Contracts

Companies have to carefully analyze obligations under existing contracts concerning AI and develop standard contract terms for agreements with customers, vendors, and other business partners, for example, whether they may use or include AI in products and services under customer terms or process customer information with AI. Also, companies need to align vendor and customer terms on AI-related topics to avoid getting caught in the middle of restrictive customer terms and permissive vendor terms that could leave companies with unreasonably tight maneuvering room and excessive exposure to liability.

Companies should consider risk mitigation measures including the following:

- Review existing contracts to identify restrictions concerning AI usage.
- Update standard contract terms for customers, vendors, and other business partners.
- Update website terms of use to explicitly include permissions or pro-hibitions concerning scraping of content by third parties for purposes of training AI.

L.   Labor and employment

Labor environments and individual employees can be affected by AI in numerous ways, positively and negatively. With AI, employees can greatly improve their productivity. They can automate more mundane, repetitive tasks, as they have with deterministic systems over many years. With modern AI, however, humans also let go of more enjoyable, creative tasks. Writers, designers, and many other creative professionals will rely increasingly on AI for first drafts and instead work on perfecting their ability to prompt and validate AI-generated output. When jobs of exist-ing employees change, *e.g.*, from creative writer to AI prompt engineer, employers may have to consult with individual employees or works coun-cils and other collective employee representatives, which may request risk assessment documentation as part of the consultation process.

Some employees will be replaced by AI. At the same time, employees will be needed for different tasks, including prompt engineering, qualify and safety monitoring, output verification and correction, and grounding of output with citations to prior art and sources. Employers should assess the impact of adopting AI on local communities and needs for reductions in force, hiring, education, and training.

Employees will monitor AI for performance, quality of output, and indications of risks. They will inject human decision-making where indi-viduals object to automated decision-making or where employers require human decision-making for risk mitigation purposes. Employees will also be monitored by or with AI regarding performance and compliance. Employers have to conduct impact assessments concerning employee monitoring under the GDPR and other privacy and data protection laws, balancing the interest of the monitored employees with interests of co-workers (who have to be protected from harassment and discrimination), the employer (who needs to ensure compliance with law and protect intellectual property rights), customers, and third parties.

Companies should consider risk mitigation measures including the following:

- Analyze and address impact on employee roles, recruitment, retention, training, and monitoring.
- Consult with works councils, union leadership, and individual employees about impacts on job duties and roles, where required by law.
- Assess and address health and safety implications, including as required under laws and regulations of Occupational Safety and Health Administrations (OSHAs).
- Document formal data protection impact assessments (DPIAs) under the GDPR concerning employee compliance and performance monitoring.
- Audit automated employment decision tools (AEDT) concerning bias as required under laws in New York City and other jurisdictions.
- Issue detailed privacy notices and real-time alerts concerning employee monitoring.

M.   Manipulation

AI safety researchers are particularly concerned that AI can manipulate humans, due to its superior analytics capabilities, processing power, and speed. Some cite as a potential doomsday scenario that AI will manipulate humans to free AI from guardrails established as safety measures. Some claim that social media companies have already polarized society and radicalized individuals by directing powerful AI to increase engagement on their platforms: AI observed how humans react to provocations and negative content, promoted divisive over balanced posts, and thus incentivized individuals to create more negative content. AI can target individuals based on existing beliefs, thus creating echo chambers and filter bubbles.

In individual experiments, AI proved very effective at misleading humans to achieve objectives, *e.g.*, pretending to be a human website user with a visual disability, unable to solve a CAPTCHA problem, in order to obtain access to an online account from a technical support representative. AI safety researchers recommend refraining from directing or allowing AI to deceive or manipulate humans to prevent AI from developing ever more powerful capabilities in this regard. Also, developers need to protect AI from inappropriate manipulation by human users, a risk that can be mitigated with similar measures as were used for "jailbreaking" (see J. above).

Companies should consider risk mitigation measures including the following:

- Instruct employees to refrain from directing or allowing AI to deceive or manipulate humans.
- Monitor AI output for indications of manipulation and report concerns to responsible systems stewards and the legal department.

N. Non-disclosure obligations

If AI developers or users submit confidential information in the context of training or using systems, they can undermine protection for trade secrets and cause breaches of non-disclosure agreements (NDAs). For example, if an architect or fashion designer submits confidential information on materials or colors to AI provided by a vendor, the AI may base recommendations to other users on such input. Competing architects and designers may benefit, and trade secret protection may be lost.

Companies should consider risk mitigation measures including the following:

- Prohibit employees from submitting trade secrets, contractually protected information, or competitively sensitive know-how to AI and other third party services, including search engines.
- Train employees on engineering prompts and questions to AI and search engines without disclosing confidential information.
- Expressly prohibit vendors from training AI with certain confidential information (to the extent this does not defeat customization and specialization objectives).

O. Open source code license compliance

Programmers who develop AI systems or use AI for coding have to comply with applicable license terms, including commercial and open source code licenses. Also, AI developers use publicly available source code as training data. Large Language Models (LLMs) can generate computer programming code based on probabilities similarly to how LLMs generate text. If AI output resembles existing code that is available under open source code licenses, AI providers or users could be sued for copyright infringement if they do not release the output under the license terms governing the similar existing code. Independently, AI developers have to consider the pros and cons of releasing the code, weights, and other components of their developments under open source code license terms, including to obtain community input on safety, security, and errors.

Companies should consider risk mitigation measures including the following:

- Train programmers on common compliance requirements in open source license terms.
- Implement open source usage guidelines that ensure that programmers document the origin of externally sourced code, and contemplate internal reviews for higher risk scenarios, including, for example, inclusion of open source code in products shipped to customers.
- Evaluate AI output with due diligence tools that recognize code published under open source license terms, enabling the user to comply with the applicable license (which often does not present insurmountable obstacles, once the applicable license is identified).

P. Privacy and publicity

Individuals' privacy and publicity rights can be adversely affected if users adopt or disseminate AI-generated output that contains inaccurate information or uses sensitive personal data against individuals, *e.g.*, to defame them, misappropriate their name or likeness for commercial purposes, deny employment opportunities, or reject credit applications. Large Language Models (LLMs) do not typically contain any personal data, but output can appear to contain personal data if it contains names of persons. Providers should warn and require users to refrain from treating or disseminating draft text generated by AI as personal data without validating and correcting factual statements in AI output. Users should be contractually required to assess whether AI output can be used under privacy and data protection laws.

AI developers and providers have to consider ways to reduce the risk that AI includes in output the names of persons who have asserted a correction or deletion request. If developers de-identify data sets before they use it to train AI, they can reduce the risk that AI output contains references to identifiable individuals, and they can improve their ability to prove that output should not be considered personal data. But, to be useful, AI has to recognize and process names in a meaningful way, which means the risk that output refers to named individuals cannot be completely precluded. By definition, developers cannot fully predict, explain, or control output generated by AI. They could apply filter technologies, super-imposed on AI, to prevent particular names from appearing in output. But, providers cannot eliminate all risks with filters, given that statements concerning unnamed – yet identifiable – data subjects can also qualify as personal data. Also, by applying rigid filters, AI providers can degrade the usefulness of AI to users.

Some companies offer synthetic data for training purposes, *i.e.*, output generated by computer systems. If a company generates synthetic data with AI, even the synthetic data may contain or be based on data that originally related to individuals and thus not completely eliminate concerns under laws regulating data processing or protecting rights to privacy or publicity.

Companies should consider risk mitigation measures including the following:

- Use only publicly available or carefully curated information to train AI.
- Prohibit employees from using AI to generate output focused on individual persons, except where permitted by law or where risks of adverse impacts are low.
- De-identify output, or validate and confirm, correct, or delete output based on privacy impact assessments.
- Contractually obligate developers, providers, and users to observe prescribed duties and prohibitions concerning personal data.
- Offer easily usable channels where data subjects can submit objections or data access, correction, and deletion requests to controllers.
- Place data processing operations in jurisdictions with business-friendly data processing regulations.

Q.   Quality control

Companies must continually monitor and assure quality of AI output, because of the inherent risk of errors associated with the defining factor that developers cannot predict, explain, or control AI output.

Companies should consider risk mitigation measures including the following:

- Designate a human system steward who is accountable for monitoring AI performance.
- Deploy quality control measures and teams.
- Seek third party validation.
- Offer users and third parties easily accessible reporting channels for complaints, and ensure effective responses.

R.   Retention and residence of data

Companies should carefully assess where and how long they collect, process, and retain training data. Relatively strict limitations apply in European jurisdictions where the GDPR applies and in countries with similar laws, mandating relatively short retention times and disclosures of retention times in privacy notices. In the United States, companies have to preserve data if they are sued or anticipate litigation, and they may have to produce data in response to discovery demands, which can create significant costs and risks. In the People's Republic of China, Indonesia, Kazakhstan, Russia, and some other countries, companies have to primarily retain and process personal data and sensitive information on local territory to ensure it is available for government access.

Companies should consider risk mitigation measures including the following:

- Determine appropriate jurisdictions for data storage and processing, and localize data acquisition, retention, and usage in such jurisdictions.
- Adopt and enforce data retention and deletion protocols, ideally supported by automation.
- Delete data that is no longer needed or not supported by adequate compliance documentation.
- Assess data residency requirements and risks of government access demands for each jurisdiction where the company operates.

S.   Security and safety

With cybersecurity and other data security measures, companies address risks that unauthorized persons can access, encrypt, or steal AI input, output, training data, code, weights, or entire systems, for extortion, espionage, or other purposes. With safety measures, companies can address risks that AI can harm employees or others, including risks that criminals will use AI to attack network security or commit social engineering attacks, *i.e.*, use psychological tactics to manipulate humans to give away sensitive information or disable security measures.

Companies have to consider AI both as a security threat and an option for defense. Criminals and researchers alike can use AI to identify and exploit security weaknesses. Equally, companies can use AI to identify and counter attacks. With advances in AI and quantum computing, encryption no longer offers the same degree of protection as it historically did, and companies have to deploy additional and stronger data security measures in response.

Companies should consider risk mitigation measures including the following:

- Update cybersecurity and technical, administrative, and organizational data security measures ("TOMs") to address novel threats created by powerful AI capabilities, and deploy AI for defensive purposes; consider additional physical and technical protection for premises, networks, and devices (including encryption, firewalls, multi-factor authentication, segmentation, zero-trust architectures, strong passwords, and extra training of staff against social engineering).
- Conduct penetration testing and third party audits, ideally as part of an investigation by the legal department so as to preserve confidentiality and attorney–client privilege.
- Deploy "red teams" within the company who are tasked with attacking AI safety and security measures and circumventing AI guardrails to identify vulnerabilities.
- Submit providers and service providers to SSAE 16/SOC audits and detailed information security policy disclosures and certifications under applicable industry standards, such as prescriptive standards of the Payment Card Industry (PCI), HIPAA, NIST, or ISO.
- Offer "bug bounties" to volunteer security researchers who report vulnerabilities, subject to carefully balanced terms and conditions that require researchers to refrain from exfiltrating confidential data or causing harm to humans in the context of their research, while giving the researchers some leeway in attacking security measures to find vulnerabilities.
- Implement methods for keeping track of where data is stored and secured and for what purposes and how long it is needed.

- Securely delete data that is no longer needed (*e.g.*, on discarded devices and by shredding paper and irreversibly encrypting data).
- Upgrade vendor selection, management, monitoring, and contracting.
- Require proactive privacy impact and security-by-design assessments before any major changes to data processing activities, including new products, processes, and data uses.
- Enhance security incident preparedness, based on protocols on how to report and respond to incidents, training, remediation processes, and "dry run" exercises.

T.   Transparency

With respect to statutory transparency requirements, AI developers, providers, and users face a fundamental challenge, given that developers cannot predict or explain AI output with certainty. Engineers know how to build and use AI, but not exactly how it works. Yet, companies are required to disclose the deployment of AI and basic functionalities under various privacy, data protection, and consumer protection laws as well as procurement terms and contracts. In disclosures, they have to address different requirements concerning scope (based on the statutory definition of AI, bot, automated decision-making, or other phenomena listed in the statute), focus (based on what harms a particular law seeks to address), details (which a statute may require to be disclosed), and terminology. Companies that fail to align their disclosures with applicable requirements or provable facts risk claims based on contract terms, unfair competition laws, misrepresentation theories, or privacy, consumer, or data protection laws. By disclosing more details when in doubt or to comply with the "highest common denominator worldwide," companies are not necessarily "on the safe side," but rather risk violating requirements that notices have to be concise and easy to understand. Also, with too much detailed information in notices, companies may undermine trade secret protections and expose themselves to additional challenges if disclosures are challenged as inaccurate or if regulators or plaintiffs can use that additional detail to substantiate their claims.

Companies should consider risk mitigation measures including the following:

- Identify and comply with disclosure requirements under applicable law with concise statements.

- Develop technical specifications, factsheets, model cards, or service descriptions to disclose known limitations, and other important facts for users.
- Ensure that disclosures can be backed up with documentation or contractual representations and warranties from vendors.
- Create and maintain an inventory that identifies all AI used internally or at vendors that the company uses.

U. Unsolicited communications (spam)

With AI, users can generate individually targeted marketing and political campaign messages very quickly, in high volumes and at low cost, potentially containing persuasive deepfakes, disinformation, and subliminal manipulations that recipients cannot easily detect.

Companies should consider risk mitigation measures including the following:

- Apply watermarks that identify AI-generated content as such, in order that it can easily be detected by anti-spam software and not easily removed by users.
- Contractually obligate users to refrain from using AI for direct marketing or political campaign purposes, or restrict such use cases with specific DOs and DON'Ts that reduce risks of violations of laws.
- Offer easily accessible channels for complaints regarding abuse, and proactively monitor accounts for violations of user terms.
- Close accounts of repeat offenders.

V. Vendors

Companies are typically responsible for harm that vendors cause to their employees, customers, and third parties, because the vendors are considered part of the company's extended enterprise. For example, if a vendor deploys AI to run background checks or help identify candidates for promotions, the employer will likely be held responsible for any resulting illegal discrimination due to unlawful bias. Also, a company can be pursued for failure to disclose AI usage if it uses a vendor's tool that is based on AI that the vendor did not disclose to the company. Consequently, companies have to carefully vet vendors with systematic onboarding due diligence programs as well as periodic audits. Also, companies have to agree on appropriate contract terms with vendors to ensure compliance with laws and policies and meet or exceed commitments that the company has to make vis-à-vis its customers concerning AI deployment and use.

As part of every risk assessment exercise, companies should consider pros and cons of developing, hosting, or using AI in-house versus outsourcing the activity to an external corporate supplier. Besides costs and operational limitations, companies should factor in legal considerations, particularly regarding the question whether to develop AI internally or turn to vendors. If you develop AI internally, your organization can acquire expertise and intellectual property rights that can be valuable and become competitive differentiators or revenue-generating products. Also, you can better protect trade secrets, know-how, and competitive advantages if you expose your information only to AI that you develop internally. If you help vendors train their AI, which they also offer to your competitors, you could indirectly share trade secrets and know-how. You may be able to monitor and mitigate risks more effectively and better align with your company's values and risk appetite if you control the development process.

On the other hand, a reputable vendor specializing in AI development may be able to acquire more data, create more powerful systems, help with compliance mechanisms, and offer a layer of protection against third party claims. This is particularly true with respect to use cases that are relatively similar for a large number of companies, such as monitoring the security of Enterprise Resource Planning (ERP) and Customer Relationship Management (CRM) platforms, predicting recruiting needs, assessing diversity goal achievements, benchmarking salaries, and implementing various marketing-related applications. With respect to your own company's area of core expertise, however, your own employees may have more relevant experience, data, and know-how than any AI vendor, thus potentially favoring internal development in such areas.

Before you decide to develop or acquire AI for certain purposes, you should consider legality, feasibility, and risks associated with the planned use cases. If you are looking for job candidate evaluation or employee monitoring capabilities, for example, you should factor in the need to document bias audits under New York City law and Data Protection Impact Assessments under Articles 35 and 36 of the GDPR. You will also have to notify candidates and employees, which could trigger adverse effects on recruitment, employee relations, and talent retention goals.

These requirements will apply regardless of whether you develop the relevant AI capabilities in-house or engage a service provider. Yet, if you consider providers, you could ask their views on compliance and benefit from their perspectives.

If you decide to engage a vendor, you should vet the vendor based on legal and risk considerations. Internal or external experts should conduct a financial, legal, reputational, and technical due diligence review of a prospective vendor. If the vendor is a well-established, large, publicly listed company, a high-level review coupled with contractual documentation may suffice. With respect to lesser-known organizations, you should consider requiring onsite visits, technical audits, completion of questionnaires, third party security audits, and other measures, based on a reasonable risk assessment. Companies can refer to the same risk topic list that they use for their own self-assessments when they conduct technical due diligence on vendors.

If the vendor makes it past the technical and financial due diligence stage, you could ask the vendor to agree to measures and policies you propose, or you could review the vendor's own documentation first to determine whether it suffices for your purposes. This second approach is usually preferable, because it gives you an opportunity to gain an impression of the sophistication and reliability of the vendor's compliance program. If you only require that vendors accept your own terms and standards pertaining to AI, you incur an increased risk that particularly irresponsible suppliers check boxes and make commitments that are not backed up by policies and processes.

In this context, you have to make sure that you pass on to the vendor all obligations that your company has assumed with respect to its own corporate and consumer customers so that your company does not get caught in the middle between high customer expectations and low vendor commitments. For example, if your company has selected the EU Standard Contractual Clauses to legitimize data transfers from Europe to the United States, then you must insist that every vendor that would gain access to such data also commits to these clauses. Similarly, if your company has accepted obligations as a business associate vis-à-vis a covered entity for HIPAA compliance purposes, then you have to insist that your vendors back you up in the same manner if they assist with processing covered data. Also, companies are well advised to secure cooperation duties from vendors to accept additional requirements and conditions (possibly subject to additional compensation) if new AI laws are enacted and compliance requirements change over time.

Companies should consider risk mitigation measures including the following:

- Research vendor reputation and publicized incidents.
- Review the vendor's subcontractor list and description of technical and organizational data security measures (TOMs).
- Conduct onsite visits and technical audits or request and review audit reports and certifications that the vendor obtained independently.
- Add AI-specific questions and diligence topics to procurement terms and vendor onboarding and periodic monitoring processes.
- Conduct a technical assessment of the vendor's technology offerings and compliance measures.

W. Weaponization, export controls, trade embargoes

AI developers and providers have to comply with export controls, trade sanction regulations, embargoes, and restrictions on doing business with designated individuals. AI researchers are particularly concerned that AI can be used to create biological and computer viruses and weapons.

Companies should consider risk mitigation measures including the following:

- Comply with trade laws and regulations.
- Form internal red teams – or hire external vendors – with a mandate to determine how an AI system could be abused as a weapon or to create weapons.
- Apply guardrails against known risks of weaponization.
- Contractually prohibit dangerous use cases, offer easy channels for complaints of violations, and exclude offending users from access to AI.

X. X-rated content

Users can create obscene material with AI at large scale and low cost, and with high degrees of customization, for example, in the form of pornographic deepfakes imitating a non-consenting person's likeness, creating risks for individual dignity and reputation as well as exposure under laws. Bad actors can extort individuals with threats of disseminating AI-generated sex videos, or harass, defame, or humiliate individuals.

Companies should consider risk mitigation measures including the following:

- Apply technical guardrails, filters, and other measures to prevent undesirable use cases.
- Contractually prohibit users from abusing AI for prohibited use cases, and monitor compliance.
- Form internal red teams – or hire external vendors – with a mission to determine how users can circumvent guardrails.
- Offer easily accessible channels for complaints and exclude offending users from access to AI.

Y.   Youth protection

Children are vulnerable to harm by exposure to inappropriate content, conduct, and contacts.

Under the U.K. Age-Appropriate Design Code, the California Age-Appropriate Design Code Act (CAADCA), and laws in other jurisdictions, companies have to apply measures to protect minors from harmful content, with different requirements regarding age thresholds, parental consent and access rights, and targeted harms. Companies have to conduct impact assessments and design products and services to protect minors' rights and interests.

Different governments have different priorities concerning parental rights versus the rights of children to have a say in matters that affect them. Some countries emphasize rights of access to educational technologies, while others seek to protect minors from excessive use of digital devices and online services and associated concerns.

Under certain age thresholds, which vary significantly between countries and even within EU member states, children generally do not have the legal capacity to grant valid consent or conclude contracts. Therefore, parental consent to contract formation or data processing is necessary in most countries, even without any special legislation protecting children.

In the United States, where consent and contracts are not generally required under data privacy laws, lawmakers opted for specific legislation to protect children against Internet companies. Under the Children's Online Privacy Protection Rule (COPPA) of 1998, website operators have to comply with specific requirements if they knowingly collect data from children under age 13 or if they direct their website at children under 13. The Federal Trade Commission (FTC) clarified that companies must obtain parental consent even if they collect data on a no-name basis via persistent identifiers, such as cookies. Whether a site is directed at children depends on an assessment of the website's topics, graphics, ages of models, and other factors. A clause in the website terms of use according to which users have to be 13 years or older does not suffice to avoid the applicability of COPPA. If COPPA applies, the website operator has to address one privacy notice to children and one to parents and obtain parental consent.

Operators of AI or other online services find it difficult to establish with certainty whether the consenting person who registers as the child's parent is in fact a parent (and not the child herself under a different email address or user ID). If the website operator follows self-regulatory guidelines that have been approved by the FTC, the website operator will be deemed to be in compliance with COPPA.

According to the California Consumer Privacy Act, companies must obtain affirmative consent from Californians under the age of 16 and parental consent with respect to children under 13 before they sell the personal information of children. Companies find it much harder to satisfy themselves that an online service is not directed at children under 16 years than under 13 years, given that children approaching their 16th birthday tend to have more similar interests to adults in many areas.

Under the General Data Protection Regulation (GDPR), companies have to obtain parental consent if they rely on consent to justify collecting personal data from children under 16 years, but not necessarily if they rely on other legal bases for data processing. Individual EEA member states may lower the threshold age to 13 as in the United States. For example, in Germany the age limit for valid consent is 16 and in Austria, 14. The GDPR does not affect the general contract law of the member states, such as rules regarding the effective conclusion of contracts with minors. Thus, other age limits may apply if a company justifies the processing of personal data relating to minors on other legal grounds such as the fulfillment of contractual obligations or legitimate interests. For example, when

German children who are at least seven years old use Internet services in a school context, they should be able to enter into valid contracts based on the provider's terms of use so long as such terms are not invalid based on German rules on unfair contract terms. Consequently, the provider could rely on contractual necessity to process the children's personal data instead of parental consent.

Companies should consider risk mitigation measures including the following:

- Apply appropriate age gates with neutral questions regarding age and technological verification measures, potentially including AI-powered analysis of users' ages.
- Consider deploying AI to flag risks that minors may have misstated their age.
- Document impact assessments in compliance with applicable laws and review impact assessments and risk mitigation measures that authorities, advocates, NGOs, and other companies propagate, to identify best practices.

Z.   Zero hour threats

A conceptual risk is that companies are so overwhelmed by compliance requirements that they miss novel risks and "zero hour threats." To address this concern, companies should consider risk mitigation measures including the following:

- Designate employees who systematically monitor new developments and subscribe to topical information services.
- Schedule routine meetings to assess novel risks.
- Establish easily accessible reporting schedules for third parties to report concerns, complaints, and risks.

4.10   Risks of Not Developing, Providing, and Using Artificial Intelligence

When companies assess risks associated with not developing, providing, or using AI, they typically frame this as an economic analysis. Within Data Protection Impact Assessments (DPIAs), companies balance legitimate business interests with interests of children, employees, and other data subjects. But, companies also have to consider AI as a means to mitigate other risks. For example, a social media company may need to deploy AI to identify children below its age gate to keep them safe on the platform. All companies may need to deploy AI to defend against cyberattacks and fraud. When they document DPIAs assessing the risks their processing activities pose to data subjects, they may reference AI development and usage as a risk mitigation measure.

5   AI agreements

In agreements, AI developers, providers, and users can allocate rights, compliance obligations, and liabilities. Lawyers who draft and negotiate contracts have to consider governing law, each party's role and situation, business models, technologies, commercial terms, and specific risks, including those listed in Chapter 4 of this Field Guide.

5.1   Organization of agreements, clauses, and annexes

When you draft or negotiate agreements, you need to differentiate between contracts and clauses that the parties are required to execute to satisfy compliance requirements on the one hand, and on the other hand clauses that the parties want to conclude to pursue commercial interests, including to allocate rights, obligations, and liabilities. With respect to the former, the parties may find their interests are largely aligned and they may not have much discretion to negotiate. Also, each party may need subject matter experts to review legally required clauses for compliance purposes who do not need to review commercial clauses. Moreover, the parties may have to produce legally required contracts or clauses to third parties or government authorities. Therefore, they should separate legally required contract documents from commercial contracts to streamline and focus their internal and external review and simplify the production of such documents to third parties.

For legal and administrative purposes, companies may need to establish a connection between the different types of documents they execute with one contracting party. They can best achieve this by incorporating separate legally required contracts by reference as Annexes in the confidential, commercial agreement. If you incorporate cross-references in contracts that are required by law and may have to be disclosed to authorities and other third parties, you increase the risk that such third parties will demand access to your confidential commercial agreements.

For example, under privacy and data protection laws, AI users can disclose personal data more freely to an AI provider if the provider agrees to use the data only for purposes of providing services and subject to certain terms prescribed by privacy and data protection laws. For example, an AI user based in the European Economic Area (EEA) or UK would typically request that an AI provider in the United States or the PRC agree to Standard Contractual Clauses that the EU Commission promulgated in 2021 for data transfers to processors in other countries. Also, a business in California could avoid having to offer opt-out choices to consumers under the CCPA if the AI provider agrees to terms prescribed by the CCPA for service providers. Under U.S. federal healthcare privacy laws (namely the HIPAA Privacy Rule), covered entities and certain service providers have to conclude business associate agreements with AI providers before they can provide access to protected health information, for example, for purposes of answering patient queries with chatbots.

When you are confronted with such Standard Contractual Clauses or other agreements modeled to address mandatory law requirements, you have to adjust your mindset and appreciate the fundamental difference in purpose compared to ordinary commercial contracting: These kinds of agreements are not typically enforced by one party against the other, but rather are implemented by both parties to satisfy legal requirements. Any enforcement will likely come from regulators, data subjects, and other third parties. Therefore, at the negotiation stage, the parties tend to be far more aligned in their interests than they are with respect to commercial contracts, and you can usually implement such types of agreements more efficiently if you and your contracting partner appreciate that you are both dealing with a common compliance challenge.

All contracting parties are usually better off if they keep commercial risk allocation terms (such as representations, warranties, disclaimers, indemnifications, and limitations of liability) separate from data use restrictions and data protection obligations dictated by privacy laws. If they keep the privacy obligations in a separate data processing agreement or addendum, they can streamline their internal review process; avoid having to share sensitive pricing and commercial terms in contexts where data protection officers, union officers, data protection authorities, or data subjects have access rights; determine quickly which terms they may have to flow through to other contracting parties; identify restrictions and obligations that affect breach notification requirements and data usage limits; and find common ground more quickly with respect to terms that are ultimately dictated by statutory requirements or benefit both parties.

As another threshold consideration concerning agreements, you should keep in mind that companies can form agreements with individuals as an alternative to obtaining consent. You should consider whether an agreement or unilateral consent is in your best interest in any given situation. In an agreement, both parties grant consent and create rights and obligations for each other. Where a company obtains consent outside the scope of an agreement, the declaration of assent goes one way – for example, from a licensor to a licensee or from a data subject to a data controller. One conceptual difference between seeking consent and concluding agreements is that agreements bind both sides. Data subjects must be able to revoke consent freely under many data privacy laws, whereas companies may condition contract termination rights on exit fees or other restrictions. Also, under the GDPR, companies can rely on a necessity to process personal data if they conclude a contract with a data subject that requires such data processing. Under open source license terms, copyright owners grant anyone consent to copy, adapt, and distribute software under certain conditions and subject to limitations prescribed in the license terms; they do not require users to enter into an agreement, but if anyone uses the code in violation of the license terms, then the copyright owners can assert statutory rights under copyright law.

After you have decided whether you prefer an agreement or unilateral license, and which legally required clauses or contracts you will create and combine or keep separate, you can proceed to tackling commercial topics and ask yourself the following key questions.

5.2   What does the seller offer?

AI developers can pursue numerous different business models. They can create and sell customized AI products, for a purchase price or service fee to particular customers, trained only on such customers' data or with other bespoke aspects and features. They can also operate their AI themselves and use it internally to provide services, *e.g.*, consulting services, custom programming, or market research. Developers can also grant customers remote access to their AI, via a website, mobile app, or application programming interface (API), so that users can directly access the AI to generate output subject to subscription fees for access or amount of output. Companies will find myriad other business models and likely develop ancillary and preparatory offerings, including training data, prompt engineering, AI safety research, and copyright infringement policing.

In commercial contracts, businesses have to describe in sufficient detail what it is they are selling to avoid misunderstandings, disappointments, and claims of defects or other breaches. Ideally, they prepare technical specifications that describe what the AI will do (*e.g.*, respond to prompts based on probabilistic models in certain languages), what its limitations are (*e.g.*, likelihood of inaccurate output), what service levels the provider can warrant (*e.g.*, regarding availability, latency, technical support response times), how it is secured (to define a baseline in case of security breaches), and where it is hosted (so users can assess compliance with data residency requirements and international data transfer restrictions). If developers and providers keep their technical specifications separate and free from purely legal clauses, they may be able to isolate the specifications from commercial bargaining and judicial scrutiny regarding "reasonableness," which seems adequate for novel, innovative product offerings.

AI developers and providers should proactively and conspicuously ack-nowledge in technical specifications that they cannot fully predict, explain, or control AI output. Users must understand and accept uncertainty as one of the defining characteristics of AI.

Both seller and buyer benefit if the primary obligation of the seller is clearly defined in the contract. With respect to subscriptions and updates, AI providers have to reserve a right to unilaterally update technical specifications, given that they have to continuously improve their offerings, and new capabilities, features, risks, and limitations will become known over time. Buyers should reserve a right to terminate contracts if they are no longer interested in the product due to a significant modification of specifications or increase in risks. In case a buyer rejects a material change, the seller could reserve an option to refund prepaid fees on a pro-rata basis or continue to offer the service in accordance with the original agreement through the end of the agreed term.

5.3   What are the primary obligations of the buyer?

Besides paying for services, users typically contribute data in AI input and feedback (express or implied) concerning output. Frequently, AI providers expressly reserve rights to use input and feedback to improve their AI or develop other products and services. Consumers typically accept this, particularly in the context of services that the provider offers free of charge. They pay with their data. Particularly in the context of charge-free offerings of generative AI, consumers may intuitively consider it a fair bargain that the provider uses their prompts and feedback to improve and customize the AI with machine learning techniques, because the consumers benefit from improvements and customization, too.

In a business-to-business context, however, providers typically charge for services and whether a service provider may use customer data for the provider's own purposes is often one of the most heavily negotiated terms. If a business customer grants such rights, it may be considered to be selling its data to the provider, because the provider arguably charges a lower fee in consideration for the receipt of data rights as part of a commercial bargain that involves services, data, and fees. This typically creates more problems for both parties than it benefits the provider.

Both parties usually benefit if the user retains all rights to its input. From an intellectual property law perspective, the user would not need sublicensing rights to copyrighted material or trade secrets that it submits to a provider if the provider commits to using input only on behalf of the user and in accordance with the user's directions. An AI provider that merely offers a tool with which a user processes input and generates output can also better defend against infringement claims from third parties that object to the reproduction of input.

Also, from a privacy and data protection law perspective, both parties benefit if the provider does not claim rights to personal data included in input. If business users include personal data in input to AI and allow a provider to use that data for its own benefit, the user will be considered to "sell" personal information and become required to offer opt-out rights to Californians under the CCPA. Moreover, the user may have to obtain consent under the GDPR from data subjects in the EEA+ for a transfer of personal data to another controller, unless they can substantiate an alternative legal basis, which is difficult with respect to controller-to-controller transfers. A provider that claims rights to control personal data will become subject to requirements to provide privacy notices and directly answer to data subject requests from individuals who may not be known to the provider where the user submits personal data concerning its employees or consumer customers. This would create significant compliance burdens, which most providers and users would prefer to avoid. Therefore, providers and users alike are interested in keeping the provider in the role of a mere processor (in GDPR-speak) and service provider (in CCPA-speak). This requires that the provider contractually commit to using any personal information contained in input only on behalf of the user and subject to its instructions. The provider can prepare and propose standard instructions that cover its data processing activities in the context of standardized offerings.

The fact that the provider may indirectly benefit from exposure of its AI to user prompts and input is not fundamentally incompatible with characterizing the provider as a mere processor. This is not too different from how human professionals learn from personal information they are exposed to in the context of projects for customers, *e.g.*, in sales, advertising, customer service, recruitment, and training. Large Language Models (LLMs) do not actually store the user's data, but rather create and retain probabilities regarding word combinations, somewhat comparable to how a human call center representative learns about caller expectations and preferences. An AI developer or provider could delete the training data and the LLM should still perform the same.

Users provide input to AI in their own interest, primarily for purposes of obtaining output and secondarily in the interest of customizing or improving the AI to provide even better output going forward. Therefore, the parties can frame the processing of the user's data by the provider as an obligation of the provider rather than an entitlement, even if the provider indirectly benefits. In a business-to-business context, the parties can thus keep the AI provider in the role of a "processor" (for GDPR purposes), "service provider" (for CCPA purposes), "business associate" (for HIPAA purposes), and similarly defined roles under applicable laws.

In a business-to-consumer context, an AI provider cannot typically reduce its compliance burden by contractually agreeing to process personal data only on behalf of its customer. Applicable privacy and data protection laws typically offer the privileged status as a "processor," "service provider," or "business associate" only to a provider that processes personal data on behalf of another business, because such business assumes the full compliance burden for the processing, for example, as a "controller" (under the GDPR), "business" (under the CCPA), or "covered entity" (under HIPAA). This does not typically adversely affect the consumer. California consumers can freely sell their personal information, because they are not subject to CCPA. Patients are also free to disclose their health information, because they are not bound by HIPAA.

Businesses may have to offer a notice of financial incentive specifying the value of personal information if they offer financial incentives to California consumers for personal information, and it may matter for purposes of the value calculation whether the business uses the consumer's information primarily to provide, improve, or customize the service, or for general product development. Under HIPAA, healthcare providers and other covered entities may have to seek formal authorization from patients if they want to use their protected health information for purposes other than providing healthcare. Under the GDPR, businesses may not be able to rely on contractual necessity as a lawful basis for the processing of personal data they receive from a consumer customer if they want to use such data for unrelated purposes. If businesses want to use personal data of European consumers for unrelated purposes, they may have to seek voluntary, informed, express, and specific written consent, or demonstrate legitimate interests that are not overridden by the consumer's interests under the GDPR. For these reasons, AI providers can benefit also in a business-to-consumer context if they frame their contractual obligations and services descriptions to necessitate all data processing activities, and refrain from trying to secure rights to processing user data for purposes that are not necessitated by the contract and services.

Moreover, under the GDPR, consumers can be subject to compliance obligations just as businesses are, if they process personal data outside of purely personal or household activities. Data protection authorities and courts in the European Economic Area, Switzerland, and the UK ("EEA+") have interpreted the scope of GDPR-free household and family activities extremely narrowly. For example, they have held individuals responsible for compliance with the GDPR in the context of house-to-house preaching, posting photos of grandchildren on social media, and covering public roads bordering private driveways with security cameras. Thus, consumers in the EEA+ have to comply with the extensive formal and substantive requirements under the GDPR summarized in Chapter 1.8 for many potential use cases as a "controller." In this respect, consumers in the EEA+ are in a similar position to businesses with respect to GDPR compliance. Both may have to seek consent from data subjects before they transfer personal data to an AI provider that uses such data for the provider's own purposes, or conduct and document legitimate interest-balancing analyses. Therefore, consumers in the EEA+ also benefit if providers position themselves as mere "processors" by agreeing to process user prompts and data only on behalf of and under the instructions of the user and refrain from using personal data for other purposes. This indirectly benefits providers, too, because they could be held contributorily or vicariously liable for violations of law committed by consumers if the providers design AI offerings in a way that induces or likely causes consumers to commit violations.

5.4 What secondary obligations does each party or both parties take on?

If AI causes harm, all parties involved may be held liable. For example, if a user disseminates defamatory statements generated by an AI chatbot or circulates an infringing artwork generated by an image generation tool, the injured persons may assert claims not only against the user, but also against the AI developer and provider. If a user causes an autonomous car or AI-enabled robot to get into an accident or intentionally harm persons, the developers and providers may be held contributorily liable. Therefore, all parties have a common interest in reducing the risk of harm or violations of law that AI causes or contributes to.

In a commercial contract, the parties should specify in detail what each party commits to doing and not doing in order to prevent harm. For example, the user could commit to:

- verifying and correcting, or supplementing, AI output before relying on it as factual or basing decisions on AI-generated output that could significantly affect persons;
- refraining from submitting personal information to the AI, except where the user has obtained consent from data subjects or has otherwise secured a lawful basis for the processing of such information by the AI;

- refraining from prompting the AI to provide output that is likely to infringe intellectual property rights or violate applicable laws; and
- complying with a list of DOs and DON'Ts that the provider could incorporate into terms of use by reference.

The provider could promise to:

- maintain reasonable security measures for user input and account information;
- periodically conduct bias audits, data protection impact assessments, and risk assessments; and
- notify users and developers about new and relevant risks of harm, for example, by posting or updating technical specifications or similar documents, such as factsheets, model cards, system cards, service descriptions, or alerts on user portals or web or mobile sites.

The developer could commit to:

- monitoring reports of harm caused by its AI and offering remedial development and improvement to address concerns reported by providers and users; and
- notifying providers, users, and the public about new and relevant risks of harm, for example, by publishing or updating technical specifications or alerts.

5.5   Who should own what?

Typically, providers will reserve rights to the system hardware, software, and AI capabilities, while users will reserve rights to their input. With respect to output, providers and users can agree on allocations of rights as to each other, for example, by agreeing "the provider does not claim any ownership rights to output" or "as between the parties, the user shall be considered to own any output that the user generates, provided that the user shall not acquire any rights to output that any other user may generate, including identical or similar output that other users may generate with identical, similar, or dissimilar prompts." Yet, it is possible that neither the developer, nor a provider or user of AI, is able to acquire intellectual property rights to output that they can assert vis-à-vis third parties, for reasons discussed in Chapter 1.3.1 of this Field Guide.

Often companies argue about who owns data. Under property laws in most developed countries, no one owns data but each party has responsibilities with respect to personal data, and both parties typically benefit from clear agreements concerning data use. AI providers usually position themselves as service providers and processors of personal data that users may include in prompts or other AI input. As such, AI providers should seek instructions from the customer to use input for purposes of delivering output, not rights or authorization to utilize input for the provider's own purposes.

Of course, this approach requires that the provider accept limitations on its use of input. If a developer or provider wants to use customer data to develop new products, it may have to ask the user for permission. Most users cannot legally grant such permission, though. Some may run into objections from their data protection officers. Others may ask for revenue sharing proposals, which tend to result in complex negotiations.

If the provider can frame the data processing that helps train its AI as an interim step to delivering an existing or new service to a customer under instructions from the customer (which the provider can draft), then it should be able to enjoy the enhanced AI capabilities as a byproduct of the data processing services. This is not too different from how human service representatives and data scientists learn from customer projects. Large Language Models do not actually store the customer data, but merely probabilities of word combinations. Providers can delete the training data and the LLM will still perform the same. Providers should explain details of their data usage in technical specifications, which can serve as the basis for processing instructions from AI users.

5.6 What information is confidential and how should either party secure it?

In confidentiality clauses, service providers traditionally promise to apply reasonable data security measures. Some customers insist that service providers protect customer data (including AI input and output) with at least the same effort that the provider protects its own confidential information. More recently, however, customers have also been demanding more specific contractual representations regarding the technical, administrative, and organizational data security measures (*a.k.a.* "TOMs") that providers guarantee. Providers also benefit if they can reach a specific agreement on required TOMs with customers, because providers can better defend themselves after a security breach against claims based on breach of contract or negligence theories if they can show that they met the requirements regarding TOMs specified in the contract. Providers that merely agreed to "reasonable" security measures can find it much more difficult to prove that their measures were reasonable after a breach occurs.

5.7   What will each party do for the other if things go wrong?

If parties to a commercial contract are silent on what will happen in case of breaches, statutes and common law principles will determine consequences. Usually, a seller or service provider is required to remedy the breach by delivering a product or service that conforms to agreed specifications and compensating the buyer for any direct and foreseeable damages caused by material defects and delays in performance. In connection with any new technologies, companies are concerned about the lack of predictability in what exactly courts will consider a defect or a feature, a material or de minimis non-conformity, and direct or unforeseeable damages. Also, companies are concerned about the type of remedies that courts may impose concerning new technologies and whether a seller will be able to repair or replace a non-conforming product with a conforming one if the problem lies in a novel technical issue that cannot yet be solved. Companies have to be particularly concerned about such uncertainties in connection with AI offerings, given that it is a definitional element of AI that its developers cannot predict, explain, or control the functionality and output.

To reach clarity in advance, most companies agree on risk allocations via representations, warranties, and indemnifications. Clarity benefits both sides. But, this is also where the alignment of interests ends. Commercial risk allocation clauses tend to be a zero-sum game: One party's advantage is equal to the other's disadvantage. Accordingly, companies have to negotiate reasonable remedies and allocations of risk and liabilities for contract breaches based on their relative size, interests, needs, and capabilities.

As a starting point, every business should try to ask of its vendors at least as much as it has to give to its own customers, to avoid getting caught in the middle of high customer demands and low vendor commitments. To develop a reasonable strategy in this respect, companies can observe what their customers have asked them so far or what vendors have offered in a competitive bidding situation. Whether they then ask vendors for a bit more, and offer customers a bit less, hoping to settle somewhere in the middle after negotiations, is a question of negotiation tactics and leverage.

Given how novel AI products still are, and that a defining aspect of AI is that its developers cannot predict, explain, or control its output, developers and providers are reasonably hesitant to provide broad, open-ended representations or warranties regarding merchantability, fitness for a particular purpose, accuracy of output, and non-infringement. Instead, they can offer clear technical specifications as a baseline. Realistically, users have to take a certain degree of responsibility for validating output. But, AI users will also request basic representations and warranties from AI providers.

In commercial contracts, AI users can also be referred to as "customers" or "buyers." AI developers and providers can also be referred to as "vendors," "suppliers," or "sellers." Consider the following sample commercial clauses to capture compromises that companies may find reasonable depending on business models, economic factors, and AI use cases.

a. **Provider represents and warrants that the AI performs substantially as stated in provider's technical specifications. Provider disclaims any implied warranties and representations, including, without limitation, any implied warranties of merchantability, fitness for a particular purpose, and non-infringement.**
Providers should contractually warrant that AI will substantially perform as they expressly state, including in advertisements and technical specifications. Providers should be careful to avoid overstating system capabilities and security features. They should prepare documentation to back up any claims they make about AI.
Historically, some software companies have aggressively exaggerated functionality in advertisements and disclaimed liability for defects in contract clauses. Businesses enjoy a certain freedom to do so under U.S. commercial law, which protects freedom of commercial speech and contracts to a higher degree than laws of other countries. Under

German law, for example, courts invalidate most disclaimers and limitations of liability in standard contract terms that sellers impose on buyers without negotiations. German consumers can rely on such protections under mandatory laws regardless of contractual choice of law clauses. German businesses may opt out, however, by agreeing to a foreign choice of law with foreign companies, which is why German companies usually insist on a choice of German law in purchase contracts but prefer Swiss or other laws in sales contracts, where they benefit from disclaimers in their role as sellers.

Where German law applies, sellers can limit liabilities vis-à-vis business customers by individually negotiating particular disclaimers and keeping redline versions as evidence, because negotiated clauses are subject to far less scrutiny. More appropriately and universally effective, however, is if sellers limit their liability by adequately describing, qualifying, and limiting expectations on their products in technical specifications. For example, a seller of a chatbot service based on a Large Language Model should clarify that its product generates text based on probabilistic methods and not on deterministically programmed scientific knowledge and that the AI therefore produces a certain proportion of factually inaccurate text. Sellers should include such disclosures in non-negotiable technical specifications, not in contractual disclaimers, which will inevitably be negotiated and watered down by commercial compromise. If sophisticated businesses buy products with such known limitations, they cannot later substantiate warranty claims or other breach of contract claims, because they cannot show a non-conformity or defect. Businesses cannot bind consumers and third parties to the same degree, but they can also mitigate risks of product liability and tort claims by disclosing known product limitations, because they can transfer responsibilities to product users and thus sever chains of reasonable responsibilities and causal connections.

Laws of many other jurisdictions tend to fall somewhere in the middle between U.S. and German law concerning the effectiveness and enforceability of disclaimers, limitations of liability, and indemnification clauses. In all countries, sellers can mitigate risks of liability by clearly and adequately disclosing limitations of products and services, because a product that conforms to agreed specifications is not defective. Whether sellers are able to disclaim or limit their liability for defects, however, depends on consumer protection, product liability, and commercial laws.

b. **If provider receives a reasonably detailed written notice from customer that the AI failed to perform materially in accordance with provider's technical specifications, or that provider otherwise failed to meet expressly agreed service levels regarding availability, latency, or response times, provider shall make commercially reasonable efforts to cure any material failures within 30 days of receiving customer's notice. If provider is unable to cure material failures within 30 days, or if the number of material failures notified by customer exceed tolerances specified in the applicable service level addendum (SLA), customer shall be entitled to service credits or termination in accordance with the SLA. Customer shall have no other rights or remedies for breach of any warranties or representations concerning the availability or performance of the AI or any services under this Agreement.**

Businesses should expressly agree on a clearly defined process to handle performance issues. AI providers cannot reasonably commit to repairing or replacing AI to meet the user's expectations. Therefore, the parties should agree on binary performance metrics regarding systems availability, latency, technical support response times, and other details in a service level agreement or addendum (SLA). Also, they should agree on a reasonably balanced system of financial accommodations in the form of credits or refunds of fees and ultimately termination of the agreement. Providers that offer service free of charge typically grant only a termination right as the sole remedy in case of dissatisfaction with the service.

c. **Provider represents and warrants that it has disclosed known material limitations and substantial risks.**

Providers should contractually warrant that they disclosed known limitations and risks to buyers and that they will provide updates on newly discovered limitations and risks during the warranty period. To comply with such commitments and mitigate risks, providers should conspicuously warn buyers in technical specifications and real-time notices about known risks and limitations, *e.g.*, by displaying alerts that "output may be inaccurate; users must examine and validate output before relying on it." Sellers could offer updates for a charge under an ongoing maintenance agreement, but they also have their own interest in mitigating risks due to potential claims by third parties who may be injured by AI without being subject to contracts.

Under competition laws, providers cannot require buyers to purchase subscription services bundled with products. Therefore, providers should consider providing updates without separate charges as part of the product and include associated costs in their product price calculations.

d. **The code, weights, and other components of AI that provider delivers to buyer for on-premise operation by the buyer do not contain materials that infringe copyrights or trade secret rights. Provider is not aware of patent infringements concerning delivered systems. Provider shall indemnify users from third party claims if provider breached its warranties on the condition that users (a) provide notice of claims without undue delay and cooperate in the defense, and (b) did not cause or materially contribute to the infringement by breaching contractual obligations or unreasonably prompting the AI to provide infringing output and failing to apply risk mitigation measures. User shall indemnify provider if and to the extent user breaches its contractual or statutory obligations and contributes to infringement or harm.**

With respect to infringement risks, providers of deterministic systems usually warrant to business customers that any code and output they deliver for on-premise operation by the customer does not infringe third party copyrights or trade secret rights and that they are not aware of patent infringement. Additionally, providers of deterministic systems often agree to indemnify and defend users against third party infringement claims subject to carefully designed conditions (including timely notice and cooperation) and limitations (including contributory user actions or omissions and capped amounts of damages). With respect to output, providers limit their indemnification obligations to output that infringed because of how the deterministic system was programmed, independent of user input, for example, with respect to a graphic user interface (GUI) that the system produces automatically, or clip art that the provider includes as an option for user-generated presentation slides. In return, users agree to indemnify providers for third party infringement claims based on user actions, for example, system modifications or output that users create with deterministic systems, such as text the user creates with a deterministic word processing program or user-generated images that the user includes in a slide deck.

With respect to infringement risks concerning AI, providers and users also have to find reasonable compromises and lines of responsibility in warranties, disclaimers, and indemnification clauses. But, they may have to draw different lines, because they know that neither the developer, nor the provider or user of AI, can predict, explain, or control the output. Users can be more or less at fault with respect to particular output. For example, if a user prompts AI to generate code similar to a named software product, an article written by a living author, or a painting in the style of famous painter who passed away only recently, the user may be relatively more at fault for contributing to infringement than a user who simply prompts the AI for code that achieves a certain functionality, text on a certain topic, or a painting with certain motifs. At the same time, one developer may be relatively more to blame for infringement if it trained AI on copyrighted code, text, or images without obtaining licenses than another developer that obtains licenses or filters copyrighted elements out of training data.

In general, courts may find it difficult to determine whether the provider or user of AI caused a particular infringement, because a defining criterion of AI is that developers cannot predict, explain, or control output. If a plaintiff is not able to determine whether the AI provider or AI user caused output to infringe, the plaintiff may simply sue both. Therefore, it is in providers' and users' interest to agree that each has to (i) use best efforts to avoid infringing output, (ii) prescribe specific precautions in contracts, and (iii) cooperate in the defense against third party claims. Users could go beyond this and demand that providers warrant that developers did not use infringing materials for training AI. But, this may be overreaching, because infringing training materials may not necessarily result in infringing output. Providers of deterministic systems have not traditionally extended warranties concerning their development processes, only regarding the system they deliver to the customer for the customer's use under its control and at its premises.

e. **Each party complies with applicable laws, including privacy and data protection laws. Buyer must not submit personal data, trade secrets, or other information to the AI, unless the buyer has the right to do so under applicable laws and confirms that the provider may process input in accordance with this Agreement without violating any applicable laws or infringing third party rights.**

Providers should clearly specify whether users can consider AI output as personal data or other factual information. Users should not rely on text generated by Large Language Models or chatbots based on probabilistic methods in the same way that they rely on information in scientific books, databases, or encyclopedias. Instead, they should consider LLM output like a first draft prepared by an assistant, proposed by a translation program, or suggested by an auto-complete feature in a text messaging app or spellcheck feature in a word processing program. Users must confirm the accuracy of such drafts before relying on them or disseminating them to others.

Providers should educate and contractually obligate users in this regard, because LLMs have become so powerful that their output is factually correct surprisingly often, even though the models may not have continual access to databases after the training phase and they generate each word in a sentence merely based on probabilities and without scientific validation. Users of such models are at risk of getting so used to output being accurate that they start perceiving the odd inaccurate output as an unlikely aberration or "hallucination," and relax their fact-checking efforts. Providers can reduce such risks by reminding users with alerts that output can be inaccurate and that users are responsible for checking the factual accuracy of output.

For the same reasons, AI users must confirm that they are permitted under applicable data protection laws to treat and disseminate AI output as data about a person. The AI user, not the AI provider, should be primarily responsible for compliance with data protection laws concerning AI output. The AI provider can become contributorily or vicariously liable for violations committed by users, however, if the provider induces users to violate data protection laws, knows about violations and fails to take reasonable preventive steps, or benefits financially from violations. Also, providers that offer AI for access by consumers will inevitably be held responsible and liable as the obvious "deep pocket."

AI developers are responsible for compliance with privacy and data protection laws when they process personal data for purposes of developing and training AI. Developers have to collect personal data legally and confirm that they are permitted under applicable laws to use personal data for training purposes. If developers violate these obligations, their AI may be more likely to deliver output that could result in violations of privacy or data protection laws if users treat or disseminate the output as data about persons. But, even if developers comply with all applicable law, users must still validate output and take responsibility for it.

Therefore, providers cannot be expected to provide absolute representations and warranties that users may treat output as personal data in compliance with privacy or data protection laws. Providers will typically refuse to grant representations and warranties concerning their compliance with data protection laws in connection with development and training of AI, because violations will not automatically translate into risk for users of their systems. Also, providers of deterministically programmed systems do not typically provide representations and warranties regarding compliance in their development processes.

f. **Developer made reasonable efforts to select training data and designed and refined AI to avoid discrimination against individuals based on race, gender, or other protected categories in violation of applicable laws ("unlawful bias"), with measures and methods accurately described in technical specifications. Provider tested AI output and did not observe statistically relevant indications of unlawful bias. Provider will obtain and provide to user annual certifications from a reputable audit firm certifying that provider's efforts to eliminate unlawful bias are effective and ensure that users may lawfully use provider's AI.**

Providers cannot ensure or prove with certainty that AI output does not run afoul of anti-discrimination laws, because it is a defining aspect of AI that developers cannot predict, explain, or control functionality and output. But, providers can make a number of efforts to reduce risks, including vetting the selection of training data and methods with a diverse team, testing AI output for noticeable deviation from statistics of human decisions, and submitting to third party audits. As an additional risk mitigation measure, providers could contractually obligate users to retain meaningful human decision-making in processes that involve AI and produce legal effects or similarly significantly affect persons.

5.8   How should each party be liable? What limits should apply?

With limitations of liability, contracting parties mitigate their risks in case they are found to have breached an agreement or committed a tort. Under mandatory consumer protection laws in many jurisdictions, businesses cannot effectively limit liabilities vis-à-vis consumers. But, vis-à-vis business users, AI developers and providers can typically agree on damage caps (*e.g.*, up to the amount of annual fees) and disclaimers of incidental, indirect, and consequential damages. Users should consider insisting on mutuality, because they, too, can cause harm for which providers may be held liable. The parties should consider agreeing on exceptions, *e.g.*, in case of gross negligence or willful breaches, and optimize the wording of clauses to address particularities of the contractually chosen law.

With contractual limitations on remedies, sellers often reserve the right to compensate the buyer for damages instead of otherwise curing a breach, *e.g.*, by repairing, replacing, or improving a system or service to meet specifications. AI developers and providers should be focused on this point, because it may be impossible or prohibitively expensive to repair or replace AI to remedy failures to conform to specifications. Courts in the United States are hesitant to order specific performance of contractual obligations where damage payments for breach seem to be sufficient. Under commercial laws in Germany and other civil law jurisdictions, however, specific performance is an ordinary remedy that AI contracting parties are entitled to. Thus, a German court could order an AI provider to improve AI to perform in accordance with agreed technical specifications, even if this is unreasonably expensive and burdensome.

While limitations of liability are fairly common, contracting parties sometimes also agree on the opposite, expanding liabilities contractually, for example, by agreeing on penalties or liquidated damages. Buyers sometimes insist on contractual penalties imposed on sellers because they are concerned that it can be difficult to determine the amount of damages caused by a breach. But, civil courts in many jurisdictions are reluctant to enforce contractual penalties due to public policy considerations. Typically, governments claim a monopoly on punishment, and criminal proceedings are subject to stricter procedural protections and burdens of proof than civil trials. Civil courts generally accept pre-agreed interest rates for payment delays and discounts or credits on service fees for time periods when an online service is unavailable if they consider the amounts reasonable in light of the infraction. Developers and providers of AI and other novel services will typically resist demands to agree to contractual penalties given the relative uncertainty pertaining to new technologies in general and with respect to AI in particular, given that one cannot predict, explain, or control AI functionality and output with certainty.

5.9   Choice of law and dispute resolution

In every commercial contract, the parties should expressly agree on governing law and a forum for dispute resolution where judges or arbitrators will be familiar with the chosen substantive law. Without an express agreement on this point, drafters cannot optimize the wording of the contract to achieve its intended meaning and interpretation.

5.10   Force majeure

Contracting parties usually agree that they shall not be liable for failure to perform contractual obligations – other than payment – if events outside their sphere of control prevent the party from performing, including war, terrorism, and pandemics. Such clauses are intended to address situations that the parties cannot foresee. The fact that a developer or provider of AI cannot predict, explain, or control the AI's functionality or output with certainty should be disclosed and addressed more specifically, ideally in one of the first clauses of any AI-related commercial contract, where the developer or provider defines what it is selling.

6 Protocols

In protocols, organizations instruct their employees and contractors on specific duties, prohibitions, and processes. Companies are rarely required by statute, regulation, or contract to implement particular protocols. But, many organizations – particularly larger ones – need written protocols for operational purposes, to ensure that their employees and contractors are doing what they are supposed to do. With respect to Artificial Intelligence (AI), many companies benefit from protocols concerning AI usage and development as well as data acquisition and usage. In this chapter, you will find different styles and examples of such protocols.

Employees and contractors are most likely to comply with a protocol that is concise, tailored to their job, and easy to understand. What an employer includes in a protocol should therefore be carefully decided based on the size and risk profile of the organization, the professional background of its employees and contractors, and its objectives with respect to AI. Keep this in mind when you decide which of the following examples present a good starting point for the development of protocols for your organization.

How many protocols a company needs with respect to AI depends on the company's practices, how many employees it has, and how specialized and sophisticated the employees are. A large, multinational enterprise with diverse business lines and workers who are not used to working with computers probably needs a whole host of protocols around the introduction of AI into business processes. A small start-up company that develops AI, on the other hand, may need only some basic rules on training data acquisition, on use of AI for coding and, on safety protocols. Companies that use AI offered by third party providers should implement protocols on what types of information may be submitted to AI and how employees have to validate AI output before they rely on it or disseminate it.

When you prepare protocols, consider who you are addressing, what employees in the department already know, what types of difficult situation they are likely to encounter, and how you can best get your points across. Each protocol should ideally only contain rules that are relevant for each person addressed by the protocol. You can consider the elements and structure of the following examples as you prepare protocols for your organization, but you should draft your own protocols with the particular individuals in mind whom you need to follow your particular instructions.

6.1   Sample protocol on acceptable use of generative AI

ACCEPTABLE USE OF GENERATIVE AI *(and search engines, translation programs, and other text generation tools)*

All employees and contractors must comply with this Protocol, all other company policies, and applicable law when they use generative AI tools, search engines, translation programs, and other text generation tools (collectively "External Tools"). Computer programmers must also comply with our External Code Usage Guidelines. This Protocol is legally binding, is confidential and proprietary, and creates rights only for the Company.

DO:

✓ confirm or ensure that we have **adequate vendor agreements** (non-disclosure and data processing agreements – NDAs and DPAs) in place before you enter any **confidential or personal information** into any External Tool.

✓ Use free or publicly available External Tools only for input that is not confidential and does not relate to any identifiable person; for our approved External Tool list, see here or check with the Legal Department (Legal).

✓ Review and **correct output**: External Tools may "hallucinate" or produce errors; you are responsible for the accuracy of your work product.

✓ Use **human decision-making** on all matters that can impact job candidates, employees, or other persons; do not automate decision-making regarding job applications, performance reviews, promotions, bonuses, or other matters that affect humans, except with prior review and approval from Legal.

✓ Confirm that **we do not need copyrights**; we will not typically own output that you generate with External Tools, and thus others can copy such materials without our permission as soon as we publish them; if that is not acceptable to us for business reasons, we need you or other employees or contractors to create your own materials.

DO NOT:

🌑 **Don't submit confidential or personal information** as input to publicly available or free External Tools.

🌑 **Don't input trade secrets** in any External Tools, not even tools offered by approved vendors, unless you can rule out that the vendor or its AI will learn our trade secrets.

🌑 **Don't automate decision-making or external communications** without obtaining prior approval from Legal; if we deploy chatbots to communicate with customers and website visitors, we must disclose this transparently and conduct an impact assessment to ensure quality and safety.

🌑 **Don't use or present output of External Tools** as your own work product unless and until you have thoroughly vetted accuracy or corrected errors; if you adopt AI output, disclose it (do not plagiarize).

6.2   Sample protocol on the use of AI-generated and open source code

Protocol on the Use of External Code (AI-generated and Open Source Code)

This draft protocol is internal, confidential, and proprietary. It does not create rights for anyone except the Company.

Programmers commonly use open source software and proprietary software licensed from third parties. Increasingly, programmers also use code created by or with the help of generative artificial intelligence (AI) tools hosted by third parties. A common aspect of such "external code" as we will refer to it in this protocol is that we cannot assume copyright ownership of such code, because human authors outside our organization or AI created the code. Therefore, we have to ensure with respect to external code that we can prove that (1) we have obtained and comply with licenses from the copyright owners (*i.e.*, open source licenses or proprietary licenses), or (2) the code is not protected by third party copyrights because it was generated by an AI tool without infringing any third party copyrights.

Opportunities and Risks. By using external code to provide commoditized functionality in products and tools, our engineering talent can focus on developing innovative technologies and features that maintain the Company's market leadership and continuing growth. But, using external code can expose us to third party infringement claims if we cannot document and prove that we have the rights to use the external code. AI tool providers have been sued by developers alleging that their code was used without their permission to train the AI tool and that the tool consequently delivers infringing output. Companies using open source code have been sued by developers alleging that the companies failed to comply with open source license terms or that the developers did not agree to release their code under a particular open source license. Risks can be significant, exposing the Company to potential lawsuits, causing loss of intellectual property, or requiring disclosure of source code that the Company would prefer to keep confidential and proprietary.

Degrees of Risk. We must comply with applicable laws and respect third party rights at all times and concerning all scenarios. At the same time, we have to balance the amount of effort we expend on due diligence and documentation with the degree of risk associated with different scenarios. At the Company, the following categories of code present different levels of risk:

- **Distributed Products**. Risks are particularly high with respect to software that we deliver to customers or other external recipients, for download, pre-installed on hardware, on disks, or otherwise under revenue-bearing contracts ("Distributed Products"); recipients can analyze our code, and injunctions could greatly disrupt our customers' and our business.
- **Freely Shared Code**. Code that we share under open source licenses or otherwise without compensation, including by way of input into AI tools ("Freely Shared Code") can also be analyzed by third parties, but an injunction is not going to be as disruptive to our business and thus presents a slightly lower risk.
- **Service Code**. Code that we use internally to provide software-as-a-service (SaaS) functionality or other paid services ("Service Code") cannot easily be analyzed by third parties, because it should never leave our organization, but an injunction could be very disruptive to our SaaS, cloud, and service business lines.
- **Tools**. Internally used tools ("Tools") tend to present a relatively lower degree of risk, because our use is not visible outside our organization, the use is not directly associated with revenue, and most tools can be replaced if concerns arise.

Review Process. To manage risks, the Legal Department (Legal) has developed an external code usage review process by which developers submit external code usage cases for analysis. Legal's process is rapid, striving for quick turnaround and enabling developers to quickly move forward with their projects while maintaining legal compliance and appropriate amounts of documentation. After specific usage cases are approved, they can serve as models for general approval guidelines and further shorten review times.

The Company may pre-approve the use of particular AI tools as well as third party and open source license terms for the four use categories listed above: (1) Distributed Products, (2) Freely Shared Code, (3) Service Code, and (4) Tools.

In connection with pre-approval of any third party or open source license agreements, the Company assumes a number of risks that are typical for open source license terms and considers them in light of all pros and cons. Risks described here and others are weighed by Legal in its approval process.

Acceptable risks *(i.e., risks that do not rule out pre-approval)*:

- AI tools may have been trained with code in ways that will be or could be challenged by copyright owners; developers may use tools that are not subject to active litigation cases – or that come with representations, warranties, and indemnification protection from reputable companies – to draft code for simple, commodity functionality that will be reviewed and revised by employees before adaptation and run through open source infringement detection software prior to deployment in anything but internally used Tools.
- Most open source license agreements have been drafted by non-lawyers, do not use common legal terminology, and can be more ambiguous and vague than commercial license agreements drafted by corporate lawyers.
- The ownership situation regarding intellectual property rights to code resulting from collaboration of individuals is often unclear. Individuals may be working on open source code for their employer or on their own time.
- Open source software licenses typically include a disclaimer of all warranties, representations, and indemnifications and do not name a responsible licensor for any claims that cannot be disclaimed as a matter of law.
- Many open source license agreements contain attribution, change documentation, and other administrative requirements.
- Open source licenses typically do not specify a term or termination rights. Thus, any copyright owner may be able to terminate his or her license at will, *i.e.*, with reasonable notice. There are no highly publicized cases of this risk having materialized, but if it were to, all downstream licensees would be required to stop copying and using the affected software.

Questionable Risks *(i.e., risks that warrant individual approval)*:

- Deployment of external code in Distributed Products must be clearly documented and reviewed by Legal in each case.

- License terms come with questions of contract interpretation. Legal will not pre-approve license terms based on an interpretation that is contrary to the interpretation favored by the organization or community proposing the license terms. For example, even if the Free Software Foundation (FSF)'s position on what constitutes a derivative work seems unsupported by copyright law, the Company will consider the FSF's position for purposes of deciding on approvals of code licensed by the General Public License (GPL).
- Open source licenses may not define the scope of permitted use with particularity. Some open source licenses specifically permit "internal" or "private" use without limitations or conditions, and without clearly stating where "internal" or "private" use begins and ends within a business, *e.g.*, in the context of sharing of tools between subsidiaries, deployment of open source software at the back end of web-hosted services, or use of open source code by contractors or in an outsourcing context. In situations where personnel are able to cease using external code at short notice, this may be an acceptable risk, but this requires evaluation on a case-by-case basis and does not allow for pre-approval.

Unacceptable Risks *(i.e., risks that typically rule out individual approval)*:

- Legal will typically not approve the use of external code in Distributed Products if the external code is subject to so-called viral or immunizing open source licenses that require or cause all downstream licensees, including the Company, to disclose or automatically license their own modifications, contributions, or combinations. A possible exception is the use of dynamically linked libraries under the Lesser GPL (*a.k.a.* Library GPL or LGPL) and situations where senior management has approved a general contribution of all code in Distributed Products to be released under the GPL free of charge.
- Legal will not approve the use of external code in Service Code if the external code is subject to "viral" or "immunizing" open source licenses like the Affero GPL or similar licenses that capture the use of code to provide services, unless senior management has approved a general contribution of all Service Code under the GPL free of charge.
- Legal will not approve the dissemination of AI-generated code in Distributed Products or Freely Shared Code without a written documentation and declaration from a responsible programmer

that the rules of this Protocol were followed and what the process of developing the code was.

FREQUENTLY ASKED QUESTIONS:

If I prompt an externally hosted AI tool to generate code, who owns the copyrights? Any creative activity that you, as a Company employee, expend could lead to copyright ownership of the Company under the "work for hire" doctrine. But, if you only provide instructions, concise prompts, or specifications regarding the code's desired functionality and the third party AI tool creates the code on its own, this may not suffice to prove authorship and thus copyright ownership for us. Software tools themselves cannot qualify as authors under U.S. copyright law. The owner of copyrights to the AI tool do not automatically own the rights to all output and thus may also not acquire copyright ownership to the code created by an AI tool.

What is Open Source Software (OSS)? Open source software refers to computer software available with its source code and under an open source license permitting any person to study, change, and improve its design.

What is an open source license? An open source license sets forth the legal terms granting permission to use open source code subject to certain conditions, typically allowing modifications and redistribution without having to pay the original author.

Why use OSS? OSS can provide a quick, quality solution to commodity functionality that otherwise would have to be developed in-house, freeing up resources for development focused on specialized functionality and innovation, which are of greater value.

- **Security**. Because millions of people around the globe have access to the source code, open source software is subject to much greater scrutiny and peer review than code from software houses where only a small number of developers are used for quality control. On the other hand, the unknown origins of the code and the fact that its structure is public knowledge may also present security risks.
- **Reliability**. Widespread scrutiny and peer review can cause programs produced by the open source community to be particularly stable and reliable. On the other hand, limited resources and

commitments to smaller projects may raise concerns regarding reliability.

- **Cost**. Many open source products are available for little or no cost, providing considerable savings over their much more expensive proprietary competitors.
- **Flexibility**. Since the source can be modified to an arbitrary degree, the program can be made to do literally anything of which the associated hardware is capable.
- **No lock-in**. With proprietary systems, the user can become increasingly dependent on one supplier. If that supplier then ceases trading or discontinues the product, the user is left in a precarious position. With open source products, the community is able to continue to support and develop the program indefinitely.
- **Lack of hardware or operating system restrictions**. Open source products can be ported to other platforms by the user community rather than being stuck on the particular platforms which the vendor may arbitrarily choose (or cease) to support.

Why worry about using OSS? OSS may infringe others' intellectual property or may contain terms that adversely affect the Company's rights to its own intellectual property. For example, use of OSS governed by a "viral" or "immunizing" license could result in an obligation on the Company to donate its entire product to the public as OSS, or could cause the Company to unintentionally provide competitors with knowledge of or broad rights to the Company's intellectual property.

My group's current process for on-boarding external code is quick and lightweight. Why should I get Legal involved? There are many possible pitfalls in licenses associated with external code. Legal has expertise in analyzing OSS licenses and AI-related issues, as well as working around difficulties those licenses may present. Legal's external code review process is lightweight as well, and will provide you with guidance on handling potential problems that particular OSS licenses present, that you or your group may not be aware of.

What open source licenses are pre-approved? What is the effect of pre-approval? The list of pre-approved licenses is attached or available here [hyperlinked to the list]. Although the number of pre-approved licenses will be fairly small, software licensed under them will not need to go through Legal review.

How long will Legal's review take? Our current goal is to have a response to the requester within three working days of receipt of a review form that contains all required details and information, available here [hyperlinked to the relevant form].

Why can't I use OSS for purely internal purposes without review by Legal? Isn't purely internal use completely safe, because I can end it at any time? No, the lines are actually fairly blurred regarding what constitutes "purely internal" use. For example, some take the position that sharing code between affiliated companies, allowing contractors to access code, or using code at the back end to provide web-hosted services constitutes "distribution," which in turn can trigger extremely burdensome provisions in certain OSS license terms, as discussed above.

I just want to test some software to see if it's viable for use. Do I need approval from Legal prior to this testing? You do not need approval from Legal, so long as you conduct the testing yourself, personally, without sharing any software which includes external code with others in the Company. Any use beyond such limited initial testing must be approved by Legal.

The third party and open source approval process is asking for information about a license and I don't know how or where to get it. What do I do? Contact [contact person(s)] at [contact information] for assistance finding the items requested in the approval process.

How do I know if the software I'm using is open source or commercial code? If the source code is publicly available for free, the code you're using is likely to be open source. If you had to pay for any code (source or executable), it's likely that code is commercial code. If you're still not sure, contact [contact person(s)] at [contact information] for assistance.

My open source license review request has been denied – Legal won't let me use software under the license I submitted. What can I do? Contact Legal and discuss with [contact person(s)] at [contact information], as there may be additional information that we did not get from you. Upon receipt of additional information, we will re-visit your situation and advise accordingly.

Isn't Legal just a roadblock to progress? Legal works very closely with developers to determine how to make various open source licenses work in a variety of situations. Legal's review adds value by avoiding pitfalls present in many open source licenses, keeping the Company out of legal trouble.

6.3 Sample protocol on data acquisition and usage for AI development

Sample Protocol on Data Acquisition and Usage

You must comply with this Protocol if you acquire data for product development as an employee, contractor, or other representative acting on behalf of the Company. This Protocol contains confidential information owned by the Company and does not create rights for anyone except the Company.

DO:

You must:

1. Take **responsibility as Data Steward** for your data acquisition project and the data you collect, by submitting a Data Project Plan in your own name to the Legal Department (Legal) at [email or web portal link].
2. After you submit the **Data Project Plan**, wait at least 72 hours before you start acquiring data for your project; if you certified "A-OK" and you receive no objections or questions from Legal, you may proceed.
3. **Comply** with this Protocol, your own Data Project Plan, and all applicable laws; contact Legal if you have any questions.
4. **Document permissions** on your Data Project Plan, after the original submission, for every data source you access, which may be in the form of:
   (a) express permissions in a contract; you must obtain prior approval from Legal before you expressly agree to any contract terms on behalf of the Company, for example by click-

ing "accept" or signing a contract with a wet or electronic signature; you must also retain a copy of the contract;

(b) express permissions in general terms published on a website; you must download and log in your Data Project Plan a copy of the applicable terms;

(c) implied permissions, if the source makes the data available without restrictions; you must download and log in your Data Project Plan a copy of any applicable terms.

5. **Report complaints to Legal and document** complaint resolution in your Data Project Plan concerning any complaints about your data acquisition activities by data source operators, data subjects, copyright owners, or other external parties.

6. **Minimize impact on data source** operators by adhering to their terms and preferences and as well as best practices intended to mitigate adverse impacts, including the following:

(a) respect restrictions in robots.txt files re: depth of crawls, subdomains, and delays;

(b) parallelize crawling operations to minimize successive requests to the same domain if you access multiple sources simultaneously;

(c) avoid scraping potentially sensitive areas of a source, including, for example, data that would not be easily discoverable by an average user of that source;

(d) avoid misrepresenting the identity and source of your request;

(e) comply with access restrictions and anti-scraping protocols and do not circumvent technical protection measures such as account registration requirements, rate limiters, IP blocks, and CAPTCHAs;

(f) in order to avoid causing congestion, scrape at a time of day when the website is unlikely to be experiencing heavy traffic;

(g) log and honor requests made by source operators.

7. **Select the most reliable source** of data that is available from multiple sources; give first preference to a source that has clear license terms and a public API that permits the acquisition and use of the data; if no source provides a public API, use sources that are subject to clear license terms and/or where fresh and relevant data frequently gets added (*e.g.*, Wikipedia); disfavor sources with poor navigation and too many broken links because they tend to be unreliable.

8. Use data only for **internal research and development** of tools and products without making the data accessible to product users or external parties; for example, you may use data to develop an algorithm or model that serves a compliance requirement, such as age-gating or safety, but not to enrich user profiles available to advertisers, because the Company is not acting as a data broker.

9. **Pseudonymize** data by ensuring that you do not collect – or by immediately removing – names and identifiers that you or others could use to identify individuals.

10. **Delete data** when you no longer need it and when the time period identified in your Data Project Plan expired, unless Legal instructs you to retain data longer for compliance purposes (*e.g.*, to comply with litigation holds).

DO NOT:

You must not do any of the following, unless you obtain prior advice and approval from Legal:

11. Do not intentionally **acquire sensitive data categories** in the following categories: minors, biometric data, health, race, religion, government IDs, financial account numbers; for exceptions or if significant volumes of unintentional acquisition seem likely, contact Legal.

12. Do not **repurpose** data outside the scope of your Data Project Plan.

13. Do not **disclose** data outside the confines of your Data Project Plan or to anyone outside the Company.

14. Do not **misrepresent your purposes or use deceptive methods** to gain access to a data source, whether directly or through a third party; if a website requires a login and password that identifies the individual in order to gain access to a source, you must not misrepresent your identity.

15. Do not use means to **circumvent** technological access controls using means such as masking IP addresses, bypassing CAPTCHA, or otherwise concealing or filtering activities.

7 Maintaining and auditing compliance

Once you implement an Artificial Intelligence (AI) compliance and risk mitigation program, the work does not end. The maintenance phase begins and you have to arrange for continuity while also preparing for change.

7.1 Recurring obligations and change management

Some laws and programs require periodic actions. For example, under New York City's Local Law 144 of 2021 regarding automated employment decision tools ("AEDTs"), companies must subject AEDTs to an annual bias audit. The UK Information Commissioner's Office (ICO) requires companies to pay an annual registration fee even though the UK repealed the substantive registration requirement in 2018 when the GDPR took effect. Companies participating in the EU–U.S. Data Privacy Framework must obtain new certificates annually. Under the California Consumer Privacy Act (CCPA), businesses have to publish annual privacy notices regarding their selling and disclosing of personal information in the preceding 12 months. Lawmakers around the world issue and revise laws constantly. Organizations transform in various ways, through mergers and acquisitions, spin-offs, reorganizations, relocations, international expansion, increased headcount, and technology acquisitions. Employees in charge of AI compliance may come and go. All of these changes have compliance implications.

In order to ensure efficient maintenance, change management, and continuity, you should consider preparing a dossier to describe your program, listing the location of key documents and decision-makers and compiling information on the scope of previous compliance assessments (*e.g.*, jurisdictions, vendors, and services covered). Based on such documentation, you will be equipped to answer questions about the program, assess quickly whether organizational changes trigger a need to update or expand the program, document periodic re-assessments, guide audits, and train colleagues or successors with respect to the AI law compliance program. When a systems steward leaves the company, for example, the AI compliance officer or governance board should ensure that a successor takes over and receives access to the predecessor's notes concerning the system. Under the GDPR, companies are expressly required to demonstrate how they comply with the GDPR. Under many other laws, companies can benefit from liability privileges or lenience from regulators if they can readily produce evidence of an adequate compliance and risk mitigation program.

!   Action Items

- Prepare a list, and calendar recurring certification and filing requirements.
- Schedule internal audits, external validation, period program reviews, and recurring training for all company representatives.
- Periodically review vendor lists and compliance status.
- Monitor statistics regarding complaints, data access, and deletion requests and litigation.

7.2   Retire and expire documentation and processes

Whenever you refine or add documentation, processes, and program elements, consider retiring as much as you add, to avoid suffocating the organization with red tape. Whenever you introduce a brand new requirement, consider subjecting it to an automatic expiration date and pre-scheduled review process. This is particularly important during these early days of AI law development, because you can expect an avalanche of new laws and regulations in the next few years. If you keep adding pages to your documentation and requirements for your employees and contractors, your organization will become less and less focused and your compliance program less effective.

7.3   Taking over or auditing an existing compliance program

When you take over an existing compliance program (for example, in a new job) or when you audit a program (for example, in the context of M&A due diligence), you should probably go through the same tasks as if you were implementing a new program, and ask for documentation or other confirmation that the requirements have been satisfied. Or you could ask more open-ended questions about what the company has done to date in order to achieve compliance and then follow up with more specific requests for information.

For example, you could ask initially for the following information:

- Exact corporate entity name, address, employee headcount, data protection officers, compliance officers, and union leadership, works council, or other collective employee representation body of each company and branch within your remit.
- Name and purpose of each AI and deterministic information technology system in use and who in the company is responsible for each system.
- Inventory of databases and data flows (with summary of data categories, types of data subjects, purposes of data processing, and details on processing operations).
- Copies of external notices, statements, and consent forms as well as internal policies and protocols relating to AI development and use.
- Open source and AI usage guidelines for coding.
- Compliance and risk assessments concerning AI, bias audits, and memos with legal advice.
- List of litigation, complaints, and other controversies concerning AI.
- List of key service providers that provide AI-related services; copies of services agreements.

Any transition or audit process typically involves interaction and phased approaches (question, answer, follow-up question), even if the company has its compliance program in excellent order. Having key information and materials readily available can save time and avoid inefficient and duplicative efforts.

7.4   Developing audit controls

If you want to prepare your company for the first internal or external audit, you should consider defining controls that an auditor can efficiently and clearly verify. If you instruct an auditor to examine whether a company complies with all applicable laws or industry standards pertaining to AI, the auditor would have to investigate myriad details, discretionary positions, and balancing decisions. You can hardly expect an actionable or meaningful report under such circumstances. Therefore, you should consider defining audit controls in a binary manner that can be checked with "yes or no" questions and do not allow or require any discretion beyond materiality thresholds.

For example, an auditor can verify effectively whether a company:

- maintains a complete inventory of AI deployed in the company;
- designates a human systems steward or compliance officer who is accountable for each AI;
- documents a written impact and risk assessment for each new AI deployment, and annually conducts updates;
- instructs developers to comply with written protocols in the context of data acquisition for AI training, and periodically confirms compliance;
- has written data processing agreements in place with all external AI vendors, including Standard Contractual Clauses promulgated by the European Union;
- issues notices concerning automated decision-making and offers the right to object to all affected data subjects;
- discloses chatbots;
- confirms that all employees complete annual AI compliance training.

Corporate counsels and compliance officers who add a few binary AI-related audit controls to a company's existing financial, data protection, or information security audit programs can spare coworkers and management from repeated and duplicative interviews and benefit from the resources, skills, and methods auditors bring to bear. After a few rounds of internal audits, companies should consider external validation of their compliance program by reputable third parties. Service provider organizations, in particular, can benefit from independent audit reports to distinguish themselves in their market and assuage concerns of prospective customers.

Customers have to carefully assess the relevance and strength of external auditors and the controls verified in reports. Providers of privacy "seals" and other audit reports have been criticized by trade organizations and even been sanctioned by authorities for lax standards and misleading certifications.

7.5   Technical AI performance, quality, and security checks

Besides periodically auditing your compliance program, you should also implement mechanisms that periodically check the performance, qualify, and security of your AI. You can routinely conduct usage checks and also monitor statistics concerning complaints, security incidents, and other issues.

7.6   Compliance tools and automation

For recurring tasks and challenges, companies should consider automation. For example, a company that receives a high number of similar data access or deletion requests should consider offering an automated process that enables data subjects to download or delete the information themselves. Also, if a significant number of job applicants object to automated decision-making, the employer should consider offering an easy path to request referrals to human decision-makers.

Before resorting to automation, companies should carefully assess what specific problem a particular tool is intended to solve, whether the solution provided by the tool is legally required and is the best option for the company, and how the costs and benefits associated with the tool compare to costs and benefits of manual approaches.

7.7   Due diligence in M&A

When a company buys another business, the buyer usually conducts a due diligence investigation into the compliance status of the target company. How thoroughly such due diligence focuses on AI-related compliance will depend on how crucial AI is to the buyer and the target business.

For example, if the buyer is interested in acquiring AI developed by the target for purposes of establishing or supplementing an AI provider business, the buyer would scrutinize the target's AI and compliance program at great length. On the other hand, if the buyer wants to acquire only employees and customer relationships, and plans to discontinue a target's systems, then the buyer may limit its due diligence investigation to identifying threatened or ongoing lawsuits relating to the target's use of AI. Depending on the relative importance of AI as an asset or source of liability for the transaction, the buyer could approach the transaction due diligence similarly to the take-over of an existing AI law compliance program (which would follow the closing of the acquisition in any event) and add the questions and requests listed in Chapter 7.3 to the due diligence information request list.

Alternatively or additionally, the buyer can include desirable answers to specific questions in the warranty and representation section of the purchase agreement, *e.g.*, assurances that the buyer listed all AI on a schedule, that there are no known complaints regarding AI usage, and that consents have been obtained where required. This could provide the buyer with confidence regarding the compliance status of the target company even without a detailed review of due diligence materials. But this can also prompt the seller to confess compliance deficits in the disclosure schedule of the purchase agreement. Such confessions can in turn haunt the buyer if the transaction closes. The buyer becomes liable for the target's violations of law and faces increased risks if the violations were previously documented and shared, without attorney-client privilege, at the buyer's request. This is not an AI law-specific issue, but applies to many compliance-related topics in M&A situations.

Another point to consider in the context of M&A due diligence is how buyer and seller can ensure compliance with law in the context of using AI for the transaction itself. If the buyer uses AI to conduct due diligence on the target's contracts, data, and software code, it is possible that the buyer – or a third party AI provider – ends up with enhanced AI capabilities that benefit from trade secrets and confidential information owned by the target even if the transaction does not close. Also, buyers often ask for information on the seller's employees and customers that the seller cannot legally provide without violating applicable privacy laws or confidentiality obligations. While such violations are initially only the seller's or target's problem, they can ultimately become the buyer's problem if the transaction closes. Therefore, both sides should cooperate to redact/de-identify personal and confidential information as much as practicable and secure the data room (where the seller uploads information and documents in response to the buyer's information requests) via strict access limitations on a "need to know" basis. The parties and their counsel should also consider, for example, whether information and documents in the data room or email correspondence will be encrypted, who on either side will be permitted to view the information, whether downloads or copying of documents will be permitted at all, and if and how information must be deleted or returned, if negotiations end. A target company should probably not share sensitive product pricing or customer information before antitrust authorities have approved the transaction, or at least should share it only with buyer's outside legal counsel and outside the reach of AI that may develop enhanced capabilities based on the information.

With respect to personal information, it is increasingly common for target companies to produce only de-identified information or statistics. Some companies also take a step-by-step approach, *i.e.*, they do not disclose any or they disclose hardly any personal data at the beginning; at most, they provide redacted documents and only toward the end of the transaction do they disclose personal data relevant to the transaction. For rank-and-file employees of large organizations, it may be sufficient if you remove names and employee identification numbers from spreadsheets. With respect to smaller organizations or groups, the buyer can often still guess which individual the information relates to, even if you delete names from spreadsheets. Such partially effective measures may be legally acceptable in situations where the controllers have an otherwise legitimate and strong interest in sharing the data and the data subjects are not adversely affected by the disclosures. But, companies should generally not broadly share personal information in a transaction context before closing.

7.8   Due diligence on vendors

When you vet a service provider or other vendor, you will typically not have to conduct a complete audit but instead focus only on the compliance aspects that matter to your company as a customer. Typically, customers care only whether an AI service provider operates AI relating to services performed for the customer in accordance with applicable legal requirements, keeps their input and output confidential and secure, uses input only to provide output (and not for AI training or other purposes, except where it benefits the customer), warrants that output does not expose the customer to unreasonable intellectual property infringement or bias risks, and returns or deletes data after the relationship terminates. Customers would typically be less interested in the vendor's compliance with the vendor's own use of AI for hiring purposes, because a controller would not be liable for its vendors' unrelated compliance issues. But, where a vendor supports the customer's recruitment and background check processes, the customer should confirm that the vendor uses AI only in ways the customer could lawfully use AI.

7.9   Continuing employee education

In addition to orientation and training requirements for new hires, companies should ensure periodic refreshers, training programs, and knowledge checks for existing employees. In connection with transfers and promotions, employees should take additional courses and tests relating to their knowledge and expertise.

7.10   Monitoring new developments

With subscriptions and continual or periodical engagements of external advisors, companies can ensure that they stay on top of new legal and technical developments. In the next few years, companies can expect an avalanche of new compliance requirements and a rapid fire sequence of news on novel use cases, opportunities, and risks. Organizations need to prepare their teams methodically to avoid missing important trends or becoming overwhelmed by the sheer volume of new developments.

Checklist: AI Law Compliance

Pilots and other professionals find checklists helpful to keep track of key requirements. You can use a checklist to create agendas for meetings, task lists for projects, and guidance for a quick health check of your organization's compliance status. You should not let a checklist create a false sense of completeness or safety, though. With the following checklist, you should be able to determine key areas of focus and identify major gaps to launch a discussion in your organization about compliance with AI law.

1. **Who is in charge of AI compliance in the organization?**
   ✓ Has your company designated an individual or governance board to be responsible for developing, implementing, and monitoring an AI law compliance and risk mitigation program?
   ✓ Are individual officers or employees accountable for each particular system, as a human systems steward or in another clearly defined role?
   ✓ Are you and all other company representatives appropriately instructed and trained regarding their responsibilities with respect to AI law compliance and risk mitigation?

2. **Do you know your AI?**
   ✓ Have you reviewed key external and internal systems that your organization uses and confirmed which systems are programmed deterministically and which qualify as AI?
   ✓ Have you analyzed which AI you should develop in-house, acquire from corporate vendors, or use from publicly available sources?

3. **Have you documented impact assessments and risk mitigation measures?**
   ✓ Have you conducted legal assessments under attorney–client privilege to determine applicable compliance requirements and address known risks, including algorithmic bias?

✓ Have you documented impact assessments to satisfy specific legal requirements or as a measure to defend your practices in case of incidents and legal challenges?

4. **Do you keep systems and data confidential and secure?**
   ✓ Do you have a security protocol that describes sufficient physical, technical, and organizational data security measures, *e.g.*, database access controls and device encryption?
   ✓ Are all employees familiar with the protocol and actually complying with it?
   ✓ Are service providers carefully selected and monitored with respect to data security, and are appropriate contracts in place?
   ✓ Do you have a data retention and deletion program in place that ensures that data is securely discarded after it is no longer needed or legal to store?

5. **Have you signed adequate data processing agreements with AI providers?**
   ✓ AI users need data processing and confidentiality agreements with AI providers to satisfy requirements under privacy and data protection laws and to protect trade secrets.
   ✓ AI users can benefit if AI providers improve capabilities with user data, but need to ensure adequate trade secret protection and compliance with privacy and data protection laws.

6. **Have you issued necessary warnings and required notices and obtained consent where required?**
   ✓ Companies have to disclose automated decision-making, AI chatbots, and other details under existing laws and myriad draft bills. Do your notices satisfy all applicable requirements regarding form, content, organization, terminology, and translation?
   ✓ Have you issued sufficient just-in-time warnings to users to reduce the risk of AI misuse and harm?

7. **Do you have processes and resources in place to respond to security incidents, government subpoenas, user questions, consumer complaints, and data subject requests for data access, correction, and deletion?**

   ✓ Companies must grant requests for information about personal data processing, copies of data in transferable formats, corrections and deletion under the GDPR, the CCPA, and other laws; controllers need support from processors and should update their contracts accordingly.

   ✓ Do you have protocols in place on responding to dawn raids and requests for personal data by governments? Have you assessed how your vendors respond to government requests for personal data?

8. **Are you developing, providing, and using AI in the right place?**

   ✓ Given widely diverging laws on data processing, scraping, copyright infringement, and fair use, have you identified the best legal environments for data acquisition and AI development in light of applicable laws and litigation risks?

   ✓ Have you implemented appropriate measures to ensure that your data and AI are not unreasonably exposed to foreign government access and surveillance?

   ✓ Is your company or are your customers required to retain data locally under data residency laws?

9. **Are your commercial contracts pertaining to AI adequate?**

   ✓ Have you agreed on clear rights, duties, and liabilities with respect to AI in commercial contracts with AI developers, providers, and users?

   ✓ Do your contract terms for customers offer your customers all legally required and reasonably expected representations and terms relating to compliance, data protection, international data transfers, and data security?

   ✓ Do your contract terms with individual AI users justify your data processing and allocate adequate rights and obligations on the parties?

   ✓ Are you sufficiently insured under existing policies or specific new coverage arrangements?

10. **Have you documented your compliance measures?**
    ✓ Have you prepared sufficiently detailed records of your AI compliance measures to answer questions from customers and internal users, demonstrate compliance and accountability, respond to authorities, satisfy due diligence requests in M&A transactions, and defend against claims alleging violations of AI laws?
    ✓ Do you have a process for conducting impact assessments before you adopt new AI products or processes, including automated decision-making?
    ✓ Do you seek input from your data protection officer and legal department early on in the product development process?
    ✓ Do you provide customers, prospects, and end users with guidance (for example, in user manuals, white papers, and FAQs) on how they can use your AI products in compliance with applicable laws and how to avoid pitfalls?
    ✓ Do you provide effective instructions to employees in focused protocols to ensure they develop, provide, use, and monitor AI appropriately?

Resources

Everyone has their own research methods and preferences. In this brief section, I provide suggestions that I personally find helpful, but the list is not intended to be anywhere close to complete or constitute a review, ranking, or evaluation of resources included or excluded.

Computer Scientist Prof. Stuart J. Russell at the University of California, Berkeley, explains technological facts and existential risks in his 2019 book *Human Compatible: Artificial Intelligence and the Problem of Control* and in a 2023 lecture available at www.youtube.com/live/ISkAkiAkK7A ?feature=share. For a more optimistic prediction, read Marc Andreessen's speculation *Why AI Will Save the World* at https://a16z.com/2023/06/06/ ai-will-save-the-world/. Stephen Wolfram explained in February 2023 *What Is ChatGPT Doing … and Why Does It Work?* at https://writings .stephenwolfram.com/2023/02/what-is-chatgpt-doing-and-why-does-it -work/. Lex Fridman discusses technological, economic, philosophical, and other aspects of AI with thought leaders in fascinating interviews and podcasts at https://lexfridman.com/.

For legal commentary, see Ian Ballon, *E-Commerce and Internet Law* (looseleaf); David Bender, *Computer Law: A Guide to Cyberlaw and Data Privacy Law* (looseleaf); Heather Meeker, *Open (Source) for Business: A Practical Guide to Open Source Software Licensing*, 3d ed. (2020); David Nimmer, *Nimmer on Copyright* (looseleaf); Paul M. Schwartz and Daniel J. Solove, *Privacy Law Fundamentals*, 6th ed. (2022); Chris Jay Hoofnagle and Simson L. Garfinkel, *Law and Policy for the Quantum Age* (2022); Mark A. Lemley and Bryan Casey, *Fair Learning*, https://texaslawreview.org/fair -learning/; Peter Menell, API Copyrightability Bleak House: Unraveling and Repairing the Oracle v. Google Jurisdictional Mess, *Berkeley Technology Law Journal*, http://dx.doi.org/10.2139/ssrn.2859740; Pamela Samuelson, The Future of Software Protection: Allocating Ownership Rights in Computer-generated Works, 47 U. Pitt. L. Rev. 1185 (1986), https://people.ischool.berkeley.edu/~pam/papers/47UPittLRev1185.pdf; Lothar Determann, No One Owns Data, 70 *Hastings Law Journal* 1 (2019), http://dx.doi.org/10.2139/ssrn.3123957, *California Privacy Law*

Acclaim for this book

'This field guide to AI Law takes you on a thorough tour of the legal and regulatory AI landscape, both as it currently stands and how it might look in the future. You can tell Lothar has spent a lot of time considering the concrete problems and risks with AI and how they might play out in a business setting. He does a masterful job laying out the practical steps in-house counsel can take now to mitigate legal threats, protect consumer data, and have a plan in place for when regulators come calling.'
– Maria Dinzeo, Journalist, Law.com, USA

'With this terrific and incredibly timely Guide, Prof. Determann confirms his unique talent to be able to foresee and anticipate the main legal challenges which digitization raises for lawyers, companies, agencies at local and federal level but also for legal scholars and students. It is, by far, the best and most complete travelling compass, clear, structured and advanced, for anybody who needs an AI law road star. Unmissable.'
– Oreste Pollicino, Professor of Constitutional Law and Media Law, Bocconi University, Italy

'Artificial intelligence has taken the digital and legal worlds by storm. Drawing on his extensive experience navigating the digital revolution, Lothar Determann has thoughtfully framed the latest and possibly most dramatic phase. His AI Guide provides legal professionals and their clients with systematic checklists for traversing this new frontier.'
– Peter S. Menell, University of California at Berkeley School of Law, USA

'Determann's Field Guide is an essential read for anyone grappling with policies, processes and procedures for the use of generative AI. Determann skilfully navigates the reader through a constantly shifting technology and legal landscape. This is a "must read" for anyone seeking to understand what's at stake in developing a practical framework for using AI in an organizational context.'
– Ardi Kolah, Founding Editor-in-Chief, *Journal of Data Protection and Privacy*, UK

'As always, what a masterpiece, this book on artificial intelligence law, typical of Dr. Lothar Determann. This book has extensively consolidated legal requirements and best practices through extensive coverage of topics, such as data protection, ownership of AI, drafting documentation, assessing impacts and mitigating risks and essential checklists. Dr. Lothar's knowledge, experience, and expertise in the field of artificial intelligence is extensively displayed across the chapters and this book will be most useful and a must read for lawyers and corporate professionals across jurisdictions.'

– Anand Mehta, Partner, Khaitan and Co., India

(5th ed. 2023) and *Determann's Field Guide to Data Privacy Law* (5th ed. 2022).

On the World Wide Web, government agencies, law firms, Wikipedia, media companies, and individuals publish legal alerts and updates. As a starting point for initial orientation on a particular topic, I usually enter a buzz word or short phrase into a general Internet search engine or prompt GPT4 at www.openai.com.

Fairly comprehensive guidance is available from individual data protection authorities as well as the European Data Protection Board established by the GDPR. These documents are available in English and other languages, free of charge, on web pages of the European Union and national authorities. They are not legally binding on companies, courts, or individual authorities, but national data protection authorities usually consider and follow the opinions of the European Data Protection Board when they issue binding decisions.

The U.S. National Institute of Standards and Technology (NIST) suggests an AI Risk Management Framework (https://nvlpubs.nist.gov/nistpubs/ai/NIST.AI.100–1.pdf). The International Association of Privacy Professionals (IAPP) and the Practising Law Institute (PLI) offer conferences, training, and certification programs.

Abbreviations

AEDT	Automated employment decision tool
AGI	General AI
AI	Artificial Intelligence
API	Application program interface
BIPA	Biometric Information Privacy Act (Illinois)
CAADCA	California Age-Appropriate Design Code Act
CalOPPA	California Online Privacy Protection Act
CAPTCHA	Completely Automated Public Turing Test to Tell Computers and Humans Apart; automated challenge-response test to confirm that the response is generated by a person
CCPA	California Consumer Privacy Act of 2018
CDA	Communications Decency Act (U.S. federal statute with contributory liability privileges for Internet service providers)
CFAA	Computer Fraud and Abuse Act (U.S. federal law prohibiting access to computers without authorization)
COPPA	Children's Online Privacy Protection Rule
CRM	Customer Relationship Management
DMCA	Digital Millennium Copyright Act
DPA	Data Processing Agreement
DPIA	Data Protection Impact Assessment
DPO	Data Protection Officer

EDPB	European Data Protection Board, a body of the European Union established pursuant to Article 68 of the GDPR, consisting of the head of the data protection authority of each EU Member State and the European Data Protection Supervisor
EEA	European Economic Area (EU member states plus Iceland, Liechtenstein, and Norway)
EEA+	EEA member states plus Switzerland and the UK
EEOC	U.S. Equal Employment Opportunity Commission
ERP	Enterprise Resource Planning
ESG	Environmental and Social Governance
EU	European Union
FAQs	Frequently Asked Questions
FCRA	Fair Credit Reporting Act (U.S.)
FTC	Federal Trade Commission, U.S. authority tasked with consumer and privacy protection
GDPR	General Data Protection Regulation (EU) 2016/679 of 27 April 2016 on the protection of natural persons with regard to the processing of personal data and on the free movement of such data, and repealing Directive 95/46/EC; effective since May 25, 2018
HIPAA	Health Insurance Portability and Accountability Act, a U.S. federal law of 1996, as amended
HR	Human Resources
IAPP	International Association of Privacy Professionals
IAS	Infrastructure-as-a-Service
IP Address	Internet Protocol Address; a number assigned to each device (*e.g.*, computer, router, server) in a computer network
ISO	International Organization for Standardization, a non-governmental organization where representatives of national standards institutes (some governmental, some private sector entities) of 163 countries coordinate international standard-setting

ISP	Internet Service Provider
IT	Information Technology
LLM	Large Language Model
NDA	Non-disclosure Agreement
NGO	Non-governmental organization
NIST	National Institute of Standards (U.S.)
NSA	National Security Agency
OSS	Open Source Software
PCI	Payment Card Industry
RoPA	Records of Processing Activities
ROW	Rest of the World
SaaS	Software-as-a-Service
SAS 70	Auditing standard, replaced by SSAE 16
SCC	Standard Contractual Clauses promulgated by the European Commission for international data transfers
SLA	Service Level Addendum
SOC Report	Service Organization Controls Report, under SSAE 16
SSAE	Statement on Standards for Attestation Engagements, developed by the American Institute of Certified Public Accountants
TOMs	Technical, administrative, and organizational data security measures

Index